Making sense of teaching

Developing Teachers and Teaching

Series Editor: **Christopher Day**, Professor of Education, University of Nottingham.

Teachers and schools will wish not only to survive but also to flourish in a period which holds increased opportunities for self-management – albeit within centrally designed guidelines – combined with increased public and professional accountability. Each of the authors in the series provides perspectives which will both challenge and support practitioners at all levels who wish to extend their critical skills, qualities and knowledge of schools, pupils and teachers.

Current titles:

Making sense of teaching

Sally Brown and Donald McIntyre

Open University Press
Buckingham · Philadelphia

Open University Press
Celtic Court
22 Ballmoor
Buckingham
MK18 1XW

and
1900 Frost Road, Suite 101
Bristol, PA 19007, USA

First Published 1993

A catalogue record of this book is available
from the British Library

Library of Congress Cataloging-in-Publication Data

Brown, Sally A.
    Making sense of teaching / Sally Brown & Donald McIntyre.
        p.   cm. – (Developing teachers and teaching)
    Includes index.
    ISBN 0–335–15796–3   ISBN 0–335–15795–5 (pbk.)
    1. Teaching.   I. McIntyre, Donald, 1937–   .   II. Title.
III. Series.
LB1025.3.B76   1992
371.1'02—dc20   92–17382
                                                                    CIP

Typeset by Graphicraft Typesetters Limited, Hong Kong
Printed in Great Britain by St Edmundsbury Press Ltd
Bury St Edmunds, Suffolk

Contents

Series editor's introduction

This is a book about how teachers themselves make sense of what they do. Its authors aim, modestly but realistically, at starting to develop an understanding of the professional craft knowledge of teachers through their own eyes and those of their pupils. This highly readable account of a research project which involved sixteen primary and secondary school teachers, focuses upon positive aspects of teaching, identifying a number of major goals that the teachers in the study had in carrying out their teaching in the classroom. Whilst the broad findings that teachers' major concerns in the classroom are with the maintenance of states of pupil activity, pupil progress, their own actions, routines and repertoires, and the conditions in which they work, in themselves provide few surprises, the complexity within and between these revealed by the research provides clear indications of the importance of promoting reflective practice and the articulation and sharing of knowledge by teachers about teaching. The book provides a complement to those in the series by Olson, Elliott, Smyth, Bell and Day concerned with promoting reflective practice. It will be of immense value to all those involved in pre-service and in-service education, curriculum innovation and appraisal.

Christopher Day

1

Making sense of teaching: a priority for theory, policy and practice

This book is about making sense of teaching from the perspective of teachers themselves. For anyone concerned with the initial professional education of teachers, with teachers' professional development through in-service education, with the planning and implementation of curriculum innovations or with teacher appraisal, an understanding of the nature of the activity we call 'teaching' must be a priority. In particular, there is an urgent need to know more about what teachers do well in classrooms and about how they do these things. Furthermore, any understanding of teaching will be severely limited unless it incorporates an understanding of how teachers themselves make sense of what they do: how they construe and evaluate their own teaching, how they make judgements, and why, in their own understanding, they choose to act in particular ways in specific circumstances to achieve their successes.

We start this book by justifying and developing these claims, by arguing that the current levels of our understanding are meagre, and by thus explaining our own concern to understand how experienced teachers themselves make sense of the things they do routinely, spontaneously and successfully every day in their classrooms. At a later stage we shall pay some attention to how others in classrooms – the pupils – perceive teaching. In this chapter, however, the focus is on making the case for research which explores teachers' conceptualizations of their own teaching and of how they achieve the goals which they value.

We first explain how the research described in this book is related to ways in which previous researchers have sought to understand teaching. It will be made clear how on the one hand our work is part of a widespread movement in recent years to focus research on teachers' thinking and also how on the other hand it is distinctive. We then go on in subsequent sections of this chapter to explain the concerns which lead us to believe that research of this kind is especially important not only for a theoretical understanding of teaching but also for educational policy and practice.

Research and the understanding of teaching

The development of research on teaching

It can sometimes seem that the history of research on teaching is simply one of changing fashions, with each new generation of researchers neglecting the work of their predecessors and concentrating their attention on new questions. A fuller examination of what has happened suggests more optimistically that as time goes by there is a growing recognition of the diversity of perspectives needed for an adequate understanding of teaching. Thus the kinds of questions which informed the earliest research on teaching continue to be asked and investigated, but both the significance attributed to these questions by researchers and also the ways in which these questions are formulated have changed in recognition of the importance of other perspectives.

Thus, for example, one kind of question which dominated research on teaching from its nineteenth-century beginnings until the middle of this century was about *how best to teach* in relation to different topics, subjects or general approaches to teaching. The question was typically formulated in terms of 'What methods are best?' and the orthodox approach to their investigation was the methods experiment, comparing one or more idealized 'method' with one another, or with what was seen as normal practice. Today it is only populist politicians who suggest that valid sweeping generalizations, of the kind typically sought in methods experiments, are possible; but more realistic questions about how best to teach continue to be investigated within, for example, the widespread action research movement. Similarly, earlier hopes of characterizing good teachers in terms of their scores on intelligence and attainment tests, attitude scales and personality inventories are not entertained today by informed researchers, but the concern to investigate the qualities necessary in expert professional practitioners is pursued in other ways (e.g. Elliott 1989).

Accordingly, the distinctive perspective which we adopt in this book towards research on teaching is one which we believe to be especially valuable, but certainly not to the exclusion of other perspectives on, or approaches to, research on teaching. Here our concern is to explain how it relates to some other perspectives.

One important new perspective on research on teaching was provided when, as recently as the 1950s and 1960s, researchers increasingly began to ask questions about what teachers and their pupils actually do in classrooms. Research on teaching was transformed by the simple recognition that teaching could not be tidily described in terms of the use of different standard methods and that the most significant characteristics of teachers were likely to be those they manifest in the ways they act in classrooms. As a result, research on teaching in the third quarter of this century was dominated by attempts to investigate what teachers and their pupils observably did in classrooms (cf. Dunkin and Biddle 1974; Brophy and Good 1986).

It was not until the 1970s, however, that there came any widespread recognition of the need not only for systematic observation of classroom teaching but also for systematic study of teachers' *thinking*. Clark and Peterson (1986), in their authoritative review of research in this area, attribute importance to a 1975 report in the United States from the National Institute of Education. The core of the report's argument seems to have been the realization that what teachers do depends a great deal on what they think, and that research on teachers' thinking is therefore necessary in order adequately to understand teaching. As with the earlier recognition of the need to study what happens in classrooms, the need for this additional perspective seems obvious in retrospect, but it too has transformed research on teaching.

Clark and Peterson (1986) divide their review of research on teachers' thought processes into three main sections, concerned respectively with teacher planning, teachers' interactive thoughts and decisions, and teachers' theories and beliefs. The boundary between the first two of these categories, as they point out, is one which has been widely accepted and used, and not found to raise difficulties: the distinction between thinking while actively engaged in teaching and thinking at other times does appear to be helpful and important. The other distinction, between teachers' theories and beliefs and their thinking and decision-making, seems more to reflect the questions which researchers have asked and the methods they have used than any clear boundary in teachers' thought processes. Such a classification seems to make little sense in relation to, for example, Elbaz's (1983) study of the 'practical knowledge' of one high school teacher, in which she distinguishes between *rules of practice*, prescribing how to behave in frequently encountered situations, more abstract *principles of practice*, the use of which depends largely on reflection, and *images* of how good teaching should look and feel, used 'intuitively'.

It is the study of teachers' thought during interactive teaching which is perhaps most important for understanding teaching, and which certainly presents the greatest challenge. In their review of work in this area up to 1982, Clark and Peterson (1986) first demonstrate persuasively that there has been a high level of consistency across diverse studies in a number of descriptive conclusions. Thus teachers while teaching focus their thoughts most upon their pupils and, next most frequently, upon the 'procedures', 'mores' or 'tactics' they are going to use. Also, despite the difficulties and variations of definition, there has been remarkable consistency in the finding that teachers make 'decisions' while teaching approximately once on average every two minutes.

Clark and Peterson (1986) also examine the evidence relating to *models* of teachers' interactive decision-making, especially those of Peterson and Clark (1978) and of Shavelson and Stern (1981). Both these models were based on the assumptions that teachers have predetermined (planned or routinized) sequences of activities, that decision-making involves choices among alternatives, and that decision-making is necessary only when the teacher's observation of cues indicates that the pupils are behaving inappropriately. Empirical studies such as that of Morland (1977), however, showed that teachers' reported decisions during teaching were brought about by a variety of circumstances such as by pupils' questions or other appropriate initiatives or by teachers' own felt needs to take initiatives. Few decisions seemed to involve departures from preconceived plans and many did not seem to involve a consideration of alternatives. Clark and Peterson conclude not only that the models under consideration are inadequate but also that

> specification of models of teacher interactive decision making . . . may have been premature. Calderhead (1981[a]) suggested that such models may be overly constraining. Indeed, we now argue that these models may have led research on interactive decision making in the wrong direction . . . We would suggest, therefore, that before specifying a new model or revising the existing models of teacher interactive decision making, researchers should first do more descriptive research on how teachers make interactive decisions.
>
> (Clark and Peterson 1986: 278)

The research to be reported in this book was undertaken from a point of view very similar to that expressed in the above quotation. We would indeed go further, not being prepared to assume that the idea of 'interactive decision making' is helpful or appropriate in construing the way that teachers think while they are teaching. More generally, one of the claims to distinctiveness which we would make about this research is that it has been guided by a disciplined refusal to import into accounts of teachers' thinking any theoretical assumptions about its nature or its relation to teachers' classroom actions.

Influential theoretical perspectives in recent research

During the last decade, there has been a considerable expansion of research in relation to teachers' thinking and especially teachers' thinking during their classroom teaching. A wide variety of theoretical perspectives has been adopted, a considerable range of methods used, and important new insights gained. The research to be reported here should be viewed as one contribution to this broad development, although a distinctive and in our opinion important contribution. A brief outline of other recent work will give some indication of the richness of the field as a whole as well as pointing to the distinctiveness of our own perspective.

One well-informed overview of recent research on teachers' thinking is provided by Morine-Dershimer (1990), who outlines what she describes as: 'four of the most influential . . . alternative interpretations of what it might mean to think like a teacher.' She labels these 'thinking through schemata', 'reflecting in/on practice', 'formulating pedagogical content knowledge' and 'perceiving practical arguments'.

It is the first of these which has had perhaps the most widespread influence on research on teachers' thinking and which has provided the richest theoretical formulations, drawing as it does on the broad range of theory and research within the field of cognitive psychology. The central concept of 'schemata' highlighted by Morine-Dershimer refers to the mental structures through which knowledge about any aspect of reality is organized, so that large amounts of information can be efficiently stored, easily accessed and flexibly used. While such information storage, access and use is, of course, a general human requirement, the complexity of classroom teaching – the multidimensionality, simultaneity, immediacy, unpredictability, publicness and historical embeddedness of the demands upon teachers (Doyle 1986) – make these needs unusually great, thus suggesting a priori that such a conceptualization will be helpful for understanding teachers' thinking, especially during interactive teaching.

As Morine-Dershimer points out, schema theory can readily 'explain', or at least incorporate, much of the evidence available on teachers' interactive decision-making and on the differences between novice and experienced teachers. Its potential contribution may best be exemplified by reference to the work of Gaea Leinhardt, who has explored especially the nature and structure of teachers' knowledge and its use in mathematics teaching, with reference both to subject matter knowledge (e.g. Leinhardt and Smith 1985) and to pedagogical knowledge. Leinhardt and Greeno (1986) suggest that: 'the main feature of the skilled teacher's knowledge structure is a set of schemata for teaching activities. These schemata include structures at different levels of generality . . .' (75). They construe teachers' thinking for any lesson in terms of a *lesson agenda*, which incorporates any explicit lesson plan but also a great deal of more implicit information about what is to be done and how. A lesson agenda is seen as being made up mainly of major segments called *activity structures*, the schemata for which contain and relate general features such as goals but also components which must be made specific for each particular lesson. Another type of schema is for less flexible components of teaching called *routines*:

For a particular structure to 'work', supporting routines need to be available. Routines are small, socially scripted pieces of behaviour that are known by both teachers and students. For example, a routine for distributing paper . . .

(ibid.: 76)

The use of these different kinds of schemata is seen as allowing teachers to deal flexibly with the vast amount of information which is available and relevant to the teaching, enabling them to concentrate on a limited number of decisions:

> Skilled teaching requires decisions about whether to proceed with the next component of the lesson, based on students' readiness for new material and the likelihood that students will succeed in solving instructional problems, or involving selection of students to ask questions or give special help . . . In our hypothesis, information needed for these decisions is obtained by skilled teachers in the process of conducting other activities.

(ibid.: 76)

Although this account of decision-making is somewhat reminiscent of the earlier models of classroom decision-making rejected as 'premature' by Clark and Peterson (1986), the kind of use which Leinhardt and Greeno make of cognitive psychology would seem potentially very fruitful, provided caution is exercised in testing the hypotheses thus formulated.

Each of the other three influential ways of looking at teachers' thinking identified by Morine-Dershimer stems in large measure from the work of one major figure. Thus it is the writing of Schön (1983, 1987) which has been most influential in relation to 'reflecting in/on practice'. His general argument has been that professional expertise and thinking does not, should not and ultimately cannot depend on the application of general theoretical knowledge to particular cases, a defining characteristic of professionalism in the orthodox view. Instead, he suggests, professional expertise must depend in very large measure on experience-based knowledge and on non-logical kinds of thinking about what is appropriate in context.

Schön's alternative account of professional knowledge and expertise starts from the recognition that: 'in much of the spontaneous behaviour of skilled practice we reveal a kind of knowing which does not stem from a prior intellectual operation' (Schön 1983: 51). Of most interest to Schön, however, and clearly distinguished from this 'knowing-in-action' is 'reflection-in-action', *thinking* about what one is doing while one is engaged in doing it. Schön's account of reflection-in-action, based on detailed case-studies of practitioners of several professions (not, however, including classroom teaching), emphasizes the 'reflective conversations' which practitioners have with problematic and often ambiguous situations which confront them. Through these conversations new ways of 'framing' the problems and consequent possible solutions are generated, important characteristics of the process being attention to the unique characteristics of situations, the use of tentative analogies with previous situations encountered by the practitioner, and creative thinking. Schön emphasizes the subtle and multidimensional nature of the process whereby an appropriate course of action is generated, contrasting this reflection-in-action especially with mere 'technical rationality' but also with 'knowing-in-action'.

Schön's work has been important in relation to teaching because it has popularized the ideal that professional practice of high intellectual quality does not necessarily depend on the application to practice of articulated theory nor on logical analytic thinking. Its emphasis too on the great importance of memories of previously experienced situations, and on the far from straightforward use of these memories, seems consistent with much evidence on teachers' interactive thinking. However, it is not yet clear how helpful a concept 'reflection-in-action' will be in relation to classroom teaching, and in particular whether the distinction between 'reflection-in-action' and 'knowing-in-action' is helpful in this context. In this respect, Schön's ideas can usefully be contrasted with another increasingly influential theoretical account of professional thinking in general, that of Dreyfus and Dreyfus (1986), whose model of a five-stage progression from novice to expert has been used perhaps most tellingly by Benner (1984) in relation to nursing. In the Dreyfus–Benner model too, the expert practitioner does not characteristically depend on analytic thinking; but here, no distinction similar to that between 'knowing-in-action' and 'reflection-in-action' is found to be necessary. Instead:

> The expert nurse, with an enormous background of experience, now has an intuitive grasp of each situation and zeroes in on the accurate region of the problem without wasteful consideration of a large range of unfruitful, alternative diagnoses and solutions. Capturing the descriptions of expert performance is difficult, because the expert operates from a deep understanding of the total situation.
>
> (Benner 1984: 32)

Berliner (1988) is one of those who has drawn on this theoretical account in relation to teaching.

The concept of 'pedagogical content knowledge' was first articulated by Shulman (1986) and has since been further elaborated (e.g. Wilson, Shulman and Rickert 1987) and widely used in research on the thinking of teachers and student-teachers. Pedagogical content knowledge is the distinctive kind of knowledge which teachers need in order to transform content knowledge to make it interesting and comprehensible to those they are teaching. Shulman's primary concern has been to draw attention to this as a necessary and important part of the work which teachers are employed to do, and his success in fostering research in this area is as valuable as it is evident.

It is important, however, not to over-interpret 'pedagogical content knowledge'. Shulman and his fellow-workers have not claimed that the concept is valuable for describing the ways in which teachers actually think, only that it highlights an aspect of teaching which merits attention. The danger is that, like 'reflection-in-action', the notion of 'pedagogical content knowledge' carries with it the *prescription* of a certain approach to teaching as well as a suggested way of interpreting teaching. Thus, as interpreted in at least most research studies published, pedagogical content knowledge would seem to imply the use of transmission methods of teaching, since the emphasis has been entirely on the explanations, analogies, metaphors and examples used by teachers, not on the learning activities arranged for their pupils. This in itself is easily overcome through generalizing the concept to include a wider range of methods; but even when that has been done, the concept is likely to fit the thinking in practice of some teachers very much better than that of others.

The fourth of Morine-Dershimer's 'influential interpretations of what it might mean to think like a teacher' is 'perceiving practical arguments', an approach suggested by the philosopher Gary Fenstermacher (1986). Using Aristotle's concept of a practical argument, one that is directed towards action related to preliminary premises,

> Fenstermacher reasoned that using research to help teachers change their minds about the ends or means of instruction was a more defensible application of research than merely training them to imitate the effective behaviour patterns identified by that research.
> (Morine-Dershimer 1990: 13–14)

Morine-Dershimer also reports a series of investigations by herself and others, designed first to determine whether teachers' and student-teachers' reports about their interactive decisions could in fact be construed as practical arguments and second, having found this to be the case, to explore the possibility of using evidence from research on teaching to change some of the teachers' premises and consequently their actions. This work is in our opinion of the highest importance for teacher education but, even more than the perspectives already outlined, its primary concerns are very clearly to construe teachers' classroom thinking in terms of concepts not generated from the study of such thinking and to do so in order to change teachers' thinking to make it more like a preconceived ideal model.

In summary, the four perspectives on teachers' thinking selected by Morine-Dershimer as being particularly influential in recent years all rely fundamentally on concepts imported from studies in quite different fields, or from theorizing which has not been empirically based; and three of the four perspectives, furthermore, seem to be as much concerned to prescribe how teachers should think as to understand how they do think. In two of these three, indeed, the prescriptive and interpretative purposes appear quite confusingly merged. All four of these theoretical perspectives are none the less valuable both because of the positive view which, as Morine-Dershimer emphasizes, they present of teachers' thinking and also because they all clearly have something to contribute to our understanding of teachers' thinking.

Other features of the research context

Having mentioned some of the theoretical perspectives which have been most influential in recent research on teachers' classroom thinking, we shall complete this brief outline by mentioning some other aspects of the current research state of affairs which are significant in setting the context for this report of our own research.

First, it is important to recognize some of the valuable insights gained from recent research. Several studies have indicated the vast amount and variety of previously acquired knowledge which experienced teachers use. This includes detailed knowledge of subject content, knowledge of available curricular materials, contextual knowledge about the school, its resources, policies and procedures, knowledge of different ways of teaching topics, especially rich knowledge usually about individual pupils, and most centrally and most difficult to interpret, the knowledge of how to manage classrooms and how to teach that is embedded in teachers' skilled classroom practice.

There are strong indications too of a diversity among teachers in the specific knowledge and ways of thinking they use, even when they have gone through the same training programmes and are employed in similar positions: different personal histories, beliefs, values and concepts of themselves as teachers seem to shape the knowledge and skills on which teachers depend in their classroom teaching. On the other hand, there are equally strong indications that at a more abstract level, experienced teachers have much in common. Berliner (1988), for example, found that experienced teachers who had been nominated as experts differed from beginning teachers in being highly fluent and confident in their interpretation of classroom events, in their readiness to make inferences, assumptions and predictions about what was happening, in their much greater selectivity in focusing on instructionally important facets of classroom activity, and also on atypical rather than typical phenomena, in their dependence on established routines known by their pupils, and in the emotion they invested in the success of their teaching.

Increasing attention has been focused on how teachers mentally organize the large amounts of knowledge on which they depend and on how they use that knowledge in their teaching. Leinhardt and Greeno's (1986) model has already been mentioned. Calderhead (1990) draws attention to two related ways of describing how teachers organize and draw on their knowledge of classroom teaching, both of these reflecting some convergence of understanding among researchers from different standpoints. First, a repeated finding is that teachers' knowledge tends to be structured in terms of cases, so that they have repertoires of significant or typical remembered situations, events and pupils which help them in dealing with new tasks or situations. Shulman and Schön are among those who have emphasized the significance of cases in the way teachers' knowledge is organized and used, especially in making sense of, or 'framing', problematic situations in order to work out how to deal with them.

Calderhead (1990) also points out the increasing frequency with which researchers have found the idea of an *image* helpful for describing teachers' knowledge of cases. He notes that the term has been used in a wide variety of ways, relating for example to teachers' memories, to what they see as typical situations, or to their aspirations, and varying also in abstractness from specific classroom situations to broad educational visions. Its importance despite this depends on the frequency with which teachers seem to talk about their knowledge in terms of mental pictures and on the plausibility of the idea that images can be economical ways of representing complex classroom situations and storing the large amounts of information which experienced teachers use in thinking about such situations.

If recent research has advanced our understanding of teachers' thinking, another feature of the current state of research is that a good deal of the most productive work on teachers' classroom thinking has been through the use of simulations and other 'laboratory' tasks. Berliner (1988), for example, used a wide variety of tasks, such as asking teachers

- To provide a commentary on a lesson shown simultaneously from three different positions on the television screens.
- To go at their own pace through 50 slides of a lesson, commenting on those slides they found interesting.
- To describe what they saw when a slide of a classroom scene was shown to them very rapidly.
- To teach short lessons to pupils they did not know.
- To predict how pupils would answer particular items from a standardized attainment test.
- To react to a large amount of information they were given about a class they were supposedly taking over.

The relative use and usefulness of such procedures reflects the difficulty of directly studying teachers' thought while they are actively engaged in teaching. It is clearly not feasible to ask teachers to think aloud, or to record their thinking, during the course of classroom interaction; and the use of stimulated recall is not unproblematic (Calderhead 1981a). In contrast, the imaginative use of selected laboratory tasks can allow researchers to focus clearly on particular aspects of teachers' thinking. The cost, of course, is the element of uncertainty about the implications of findings in such simulated settings for an understanding of the actual practice of teaching.

One further point may also be highlighted with reference to Berliner's (1988) research. Expert teachers, he found, tend to focus their conscious attention on *atypical* phenomena, with things they see as normal being simply taken for granted. A consequence of this is that such teachers, and indeed probably all experienced teachers, find it much easier and more interesting to report their thinking about exceptional situations and events than their more usual day-to-day thinking. Some theorists too, notably Schön, have shown much more interest in the way teachers deal with problematic situations than in their more commonly used 'knowing-in-action'. It may be, therefore, that researchers' attention too, guided at one level by theorists and at another by the teachers with whom they are working, tends to be directed most towards the problems and dilemmas which teachers experience. Yet one of the most striking characteristics of experienced teachers, as Berliner and others have found, is the confidence and fluency with which they deal with most situations. Understanding teachers' thinking must most of all mean understanding that fluency of activity.

In this brief outline of recent research on teachers' classroom thinking we have not, of course, attempted to provide a comprehensive review of the work which has been done. We have instead tried to describe the context of research activity within which the research to be reported in this book should be understood. We have highlighted the following four features of that research context:

1 Recent research has led to a better understanding of the thought involved in classroom teaching.
2 A rich variety of theoretical ideas has become available for articulating and developing our understanding of teachers' classroom thinking.
3 Most of these theoretical ideas, however, have been imported from elsewhere, and are not themselves based on the study of teachers' classroom thinking.
4 Much of the most productive research has been through the use of various kinds of simulated tasks for teachers.

Against that background, there seems to us to be a clear need for research which is focused as directly as possible on the thought underlying teachers' day-to-day teaching, and for theory which is generated from such research. Without suggesting that the other kinds of research and theorizing outlined above are anything but valuable, our view is that the development of a theoretical understanding of the thought underlying classroom teaching necessarily depends not only on testing imported theories against evidence drawn from classroom studies but also on the generation of theoretical ideas grounded in classroom studies. In particular, since it seems impossible to have direct access to teachers' thinking while teaching, it is important that theoretical accounts of teachers' classroom thinking should be grounded in teachers' own ways of making sense of the particular things they do and achieve in their teaching.

We see this research, therefore, as perhaps contributing to the correction of some imbalance in recent research and theorizing on teachers' thinking; but, as the following sections of this chapter make clear, there are important practical reasons for emphasizing teachers' own ways of making sense of their teaching.

Understanding teaching: a priority for policy and practice

Teacher education: the importance of craft knowledge

Most of us, and particularly teacher educators, acknowledge that student teachers can and should learn a great deal from the experienced teachers they observe in schools. Underlying this approach is an acceptance that over a period of time experienced teachers have acquired substantial practical knowledge about teaching, largely through their classroom experience rather than their formal training. It is this knowledge which is reflected in the ways they go about their routine day-to-day teaching, and it is clear that student teachers also need to acquire such knowledge.

Implied in all this is the notion that experienced teachers are analogous to 'master craftsmen' and that in school-based components of their pre-service education, student-teachers should learn through gaining access to the 'craft knowledge' of experienced teachers. It further suggests a recognition that teaching is a craft as much as, if not more than, a science-based technology, and that teachers learn the craft aspects of their profession through observing others and, later, from their own practical experience. This is not to say, of course, that 'craft knowledge' is the only aspect of the professional knowledge to be acquired by the beginning teacher. The phrase, however, provides a good delineation of what we are concerned with in this book.

It is one thing to say that student-teachers should be learning their craft from experienced teachers; it is quite another to be clear about *what* they should learn and *how* that learning may be most effectively accomplished. Unfortunately, it is the case that the more skilful is the teaching the more difficult it is to understand how success is being achieved. Many student teachers have the experience of observing a class where the teacher seems effortlessly to have the pupils 'eating out of her hand'; the next day the student may take the same class and find the pupils uncontrollable. In general, it seems that while we recognize that there are those with mastery of some aspects of teaching, we have no coherent account of what they are masters of and how they achieve what they achieve. The effect of this has been to limit the value of school-based elements of teacher education programmes, despite the fact that elements are important components of pre-service teacher education throughout the world.

The importance of this matter is not confined to the context of initial teacher training. Inspectors, evaluators, advisers of teachers and in-service teacher trainers often remark on the 'good practice' displayed by individual teachers and exhort others to learn from them. This implies a model for in-service teacher education in which there is a deliberate and determined sharing among teachers of their diverse and successful approaches to teaching: a 'building on strengths model'. In practice, that is rarely the case. Almost always in-service has been based on a 'deficit model' of teaching. By that we mean that the emphasis has been on the identification of what it is thought teachers ought to be doing and are not doing, and on appropriate action to remedy matters. This has implied a 'plugging the gaps' strategy and research has been expected to respond with information about the 'identification' and 'plugging' processes. Ideas about how to approach in-service have, of course, evolved in recent years. School-based staff development and classroom action-research, for example, have gained in popularity, but even here the emphasis is still on righting a deficit condition.

This deficit model for in-service and conventional school-based components of initial training clearly have had only limited effectiveness. Their limitations are evidenced by such things as the well-documented dissatisfactions of beginning and experienced teachers with the relationship between the theory they are offered in their training and the experiences they have in classrooms, or the difficulties encountered in trying to communicate to other teachers knowledge acquired through teachers' own classroom action research. These and other problems, we would argue, reflect our lack of understanding of the nature of the practical knowledge which is acquired by teachers through classroom experience. Without such understanding, our teacher education, both pre-service and in-service, will continue to consist of an uneasy mixture of theoretical prescription and trial and error practice, and we shall have little in the way of a satisfactory mechanism for the sharing of relevant knowledge among teachers.

One major cause of this state of affairs must surely be the one so frequently indicated by teachers themselves: that to them most of what has happened in their lessons, and especially almost everything which they themselves have done in the classroom, is so ordinary and so obvious as not to merit any comment. To this is added the difficulty which many teachers would have in explicitly describing their routine patterns of activity, and particularly in formulating the ways in which they make their

decisions during teaching. To give an account of what one does spontaneously, even unconsciously, every day is a most demanding task which the
individual teacher is rarely called upon to do. While teachers are frequently
required to give accounts of other aspects of their professional activities
(such as the extent to which they have covered the prescribed curriculum,
carried out the necessary assessment procedures, undertaken their share of
general staff duties and complied with the organizational arrangements in
the school), they are seldom asked to articulate and elaborate on what they
do in their ordinary, everyday teaching.

For such reasons, this part of the professional knowledge of experienced
teachers is communicated to beginning teachers only to a very limited
extent, and the wheels of teaching have to be reinvented by each new
generation. Furthermore, when professional teacher educators are design-
ing their courses, it is very difficult for them to take any detailed account of
what their students may learn from teachers in schools. If teachers could be
helped and persuaded to make explicit the knowledge which they implicitly
use in their day-to-day work, teacher education could begin to achieve
something of the practical relevance and the theory–practice integration
which it is still accused of lacking. That would enable student-teachers to
begin their cycles of observation and practice with a framework which
could achieve the following:

- Avoid them becoming so overwhelmed in the initial stages by the
  minutiae and idiosyncrasies of the classroom.
- Provide them with some of the larger-scale and more generalisable concepts which experienced teachers use to make sense of their teaching.
- Enable them to direct their discussions with experienced teachers
  towards the most important features of the teaching.
- Facilitate their progression from an 'outside' observer to an 'inside'
  practitioner.
- Avoid some of the 'pitfalls of experience'.

                                        (Feiman-Nemser and Buchmann 1985)

In particular, the students could better organize in their minds what they
see in the classroom, and more fully understand the experienced teachers'
actions and routines. Their 'learning by doing', when they become involved
in actual teaching, would then rest on a much more substantial basis.

There are, therefore, powerful arguments to be made, from the perspective of teacher education, for investigations of the ways in which experienced teachers conceptualize their own teaching, the criteria they use in
evaluating their own performance and how they achieve the things which
they do well. But there are other kinds of justifications for research which
attempt to make sense of teaching in this way. One of these justifications
arises from the concerns of curriculum innovation.

Curriculum innovation

The record of curriculum innovations shows an alarmingly modest level of successful pedagogical implementation in classrooms of what looked like 'good ideas' for change. Why should that be? Many people have addressed this question and it seems that the major constraint on the acceptance of innovations by teachers is their perceived impracticality. The preaching of well-meaning theorists about the desirability of discovery learning, individualization, teaching which emphasizes problem-solving rather than facts, process rather than products and so on, seems to have been greeted by an 'all very well in theory but impractical in my classroom' response. But what would count as *practical*? Not infrequently the proposed innovations imply teaching strategies which are less complex than those the teacher is already using. So why are they not seen as practical?

In our view, whether innovations will be seen as practical will depend on how they relate to the things which teachers have learned (through experience) about what is and what is not appropriate in their classrooms, and on the implicit skills and strategies which they have learned for achieving their purposes within the conditions in which they work. These things are learned in the privacy of the classroom, are rarely made explicit and become relatively automatic so they can be used effectively (often in a largely unconscious way). It would be very difficult, therefore, for the teacher to explain in any detail why certain innovations would be practical but others would not. What teachers are conscious of, however, is that proposed innovations frequently take little account of (and may require the discontinuation of) classroom practices which are familiar, comfortable and, in the teacher's eyes, successful in achieving his or her purposes.

It would be possible to understand better what kinds of changes teachers would find it practical to implement if we knew more about how teachers perceive and think about what they do in their own classrooms. Such an approach would recognize that teachers' existing patterns of classroom teaching are highly adapted to the circumstances in which they find themselves and the purposes to which they find they have to give priority. To have any chance of being perceived as practical, plans for innovation would have to take account of what is already being done (particularly what is being done well) in classrooms. From the researchers' point of view, the information sought would be concerned with what teachers see as necessary and desirable to do in classrooms. The emphasis would be on understanding how *teachers* construe their teaching and not at all on the external evaluation of that teaching. It would be necessary to include, but also go beyond, observing what teachers do in their classrooms. Specifically it would involve an exploration of their routine patterns of regularly speaking about particular kinds of issues in particular ways to particular kinds of pupils in particular types of circumstances. It would also have to be concerned with how they perceive pupils, how they decide that this *is* such-and-such a kind of situation and that such-and-such a kind of action is necessary. The nature and significance to the teachers of their actions and what these involve would be a critically important part of the knowledge required.

This knowledge is clearly much the same as the practical knowledge we described as necessary to thinking about, and planning for, the professional development of teachers. There is, however, a third area in which we believe research on teaching, of the kind we have been discussing, is essential: the development of systems for the appraisal of teachers.

Appraisal of teaching

There is a lot of talk about the appraisal of teachers. The design and implementation of any appraisal scheme requires that many difficult decisions be made about such things as who will choose the criteria for appraisal, what those criteria should be, who should carry out the appraisal, and so on.

Research cannot make those decisions, but it can provide information which will make policy-makers and practitioners more aware of the implications of the choices they make. In order to gather the information which would be required to cover all the aspects of teacher appraisal, a very large programme of research would be required. We are concerned here with one of those aspects – albeit a crucial one.

It is important to be aware that different sets of criteria for appraisal would be chosen if the decisions were left to, for example, politicians, administrators, government inspectors, academics, parents or teachers themselves. Each group would be likely to have different assumptions underlying their decisions and consensus among groups is unlikely. What is much more likely is some form of eventual compromise which will suit some groups more than others. It is necessary, therefore, to make clear the assumptions we make in arguing for the importance of our research; these assumptions may not be shared by other groups. We are assuming that:

- The appraisal of teachers should be based, in part at least, on an assessment of *teaching*.
- It is important, therefore, to know how teachers conceptualize and evaluate their own teaching (i.e. it is assumed that the profession should have a say in choosing the criteria against which it is to be assessed).
- If 'outsiders' are to assess classroom teaching, then it is necessary to know the extent to which they can observe those things which teachers value in their own teaching.
- If assessments are to be made on the basis of teaching performance on one or two occasions, then it will be necessary to know the extent to which generalizations can be made from one occasion to another.

The second of these assumptions directs attention once again to the need for an investigation of teaching in the way we have already described for teacher education and curriculum innovation. An investigation of that type could also provide some of the evidence which is called for in the third and fourth assumptions.

A research approach

The research we are describing in this book was designed, therefore, to explore that part of their professional knowledge which teachers acquire primarily through their practical experience in the classroom rather than their formal training, which guides their day-to-day actions in classrooms, which is for the most part not articulated in words and which is brought to bear spontaneously, routinely and sometimes unconsciously on their teaching. We shall refer to this aspect of teachers' knowledge as their *professional craft knowledge* and have drawn to a considerable extent on the ideas of Desforges and McNamara in our work (Desforges and McNamara 1977, 1979; McNamara and Desforges, 1978). Our concern, therefore, was with that part of teaching for which Berliner (1986: 7) reminds us that experienced teachers may be seen as:

> models, experts, masters, mentors, coaches, and so forth, who lead the novice to some sort of competency in teaching. But a fundamental problem in apprenticeship programmes is that the experienced and expert practitioners very often lack the ability to articulate the basis for their expertise and skill.

To gain access to teachers' professional craft knowledge the research has sought ways to stimulate them to articulate what it is they value in their own teaching, what they are trying to accomplish and how they achieve the things which they do well. The research approach and methods of data collection are explained in Chapters 2, 3 and 6. Our concern was to illuminate the ways in which teachers themselves construe what they are doing and to assess the extent to which there are generalizations to be made across teachers. We had also to shun outsiders' theoretical models of teachers (e.g. as classroom managers, information processors, decision-makers, dilemma resolvers) or of teaching (e.g. process–product, inquiry-oriented teaching). It was clear that these requirements could not be met by an approach involving surveys or experimental designs. 'Loosely ethnographic' or 'case study research' would be better descriptors, but the work could not be identified in detail with at least some versions of ethnography and 'case study' is a catch-all term which requires further elaboration. That elaboration is given in the next few chapters which will discuss the differences between our approach and more traditional techniques of classroom research.

In particular, it was important not to assume that teachers would think about their teaching 'scientifically'. The rational 'formulate objectives, identify appropriate learning activities and evaluate the achievement of objectives' is a favourite (and possibly very valuable approach) in student-teachers' initial training; but there is little evidence that it reflects the thinking of practising teachers (cf. Clark and Yinger 1987). Student-teachers soon become aware that despite the emphasis in their college courses on detailed lesson plans and learning objectives, experienced teachers seem to manage well without them. This is not to suggest that the objectives model is not useful and important. It does point, nevertheless, to a discontinuity between that way of viewing teaching and the actual craft of the job. In Chapters 4, 5 and 6, we discuss what we have gleaned from our work about the craft, and Chapter 7 relates these findings to the various justifications for our research which we have laid out in this chapter.

The 'craft' of teaching

Some people have felt uncomfortable with the use of the word 'craft' in relation to the profession of teaching. We think it appropriate, therefore, to take a brief diversion and comment on how we are using the term. In particular, it is important to make clear that we are in no sense denigrating teaching or implying that it is 'just' a craft.

Others have used the craft metaphor in relation to teaching and schooling (Lortie 1975; Marland 1975; Ebel 1976; Kohl 1976; Cohen 1977; Martin 1978; Wise 1978; Tom 1980, 1984) and some of these authors have asserted, or set out to demonstrate, that teaching is best conceptualized as a craft. We are not claiming that; 'craft' is simply the best description we can think of for the particular aspects of teachers' practical knowledge in which we are interested.

The craft of teaching has been identified as an 'occupational technique' (Bensman and Lilienfield 1973) which can be taught (Ebel 1976), but which has aspects that are complex and inaccessible in comparison with many of the crafts associated with other occupations. In common with other crafts, however, it conforms to Lortie's notion that 'craft is work in which experience improves performance – the job cannot . . . be fully learned in weeks or even months' (1975: 266). In the different but related context of child and youth care, Eisikovits and Becker (1983: 96) have commented that:

> Craftsmanship, the work of the craftsperson, is viewed as an individualistic, expressive process that can, nonetheless, be taught, generally through modelling rather than academically, but with distinct conceptual principles at the foundation. The notions of apprentice, protege, and working with mentor fit more comfortably than those of student and teacher. Typically, the learner will produce work identifiably different from that of the mentor, yet clearly in harmony with it.

Among the characteristics distinguishing the craftsperson teacher from the novice teacher, Tom (1984: 101) has identified 'The ability to analyse teaching situations and the possession of a broad repertoire of teaching strategies'. He has argued that acquiring the knowledge and skill of a craft is not just a matter of the novice observing and imitating the master: 'the stress was not on making the craftsman a passive observer of skilful practice so much as it was on preparing him for his own active attempts to solve problems of practice' (ibid.: 111). In this way the beginning teacher can be helped to develop the craft of teaching which 'centrally involves intellectually based activities including mastery of craft knowledge, ability to apply craft knowledge in context' (ibid.: 110). On this basis we predict that the 'products' of our investigation of the craft aspects of teaching will not be a set of standardized teaching behaviours; they will be personalized to the individual teacher but there are likely to be certain over-arching generalizable features which are common across teachers.

The craft aspect of teachers' knowledge is, of course, integrated into the totality of their professional knowledge with all its broader educational and political features (Kohl 1976). We would not deny the aesthetic components of grace, improvisation and creativity which those who consider teaching to be an art might claim (e.g. Eisner 1979: Ch. 9). It is interesting, however, that Stenhouse (1984) in declaring teaching to be an art offered the craft analogy of the 'innumerable stonemasons who adorned English parish churches' in his illustration of the excellent teacher. Nevertheless, our concern is limited to the study and the articulation of the relatively routine and familiar aspects of what teachers do in classrooms, and with how they do the things that they regularly do well. We are seeking knowledge which is potentially generalizable (and so can be shared) and the notion of professional 'craft' knowledge is the best metaphor we can think of. Teachers' flashes of artistic genius will be a bonus.

Summary

In this chapter, we have sought to explain the research enterprise which this book reports, and the reasons for undertaking it. The purpose of the enterprise is to explore the professional knowledge and thought which teachers use in their day-to-day classroom teaching, knowledge which is not generally made explicit by teachers and which teachers are not likely always to be conscious of using. We call this the 'professional craft knowledge' of teachers and we have explained why we do so. The chapter has sought first to show how this research relates to other research in teaching and especially to the widespread development in recent years of research on teachers' thinking. Thus it was pointed out that much of this research has depended on theoretical frameworks imported from other contexts, or on the use of simulated tasks or contexts instead of teachers' ordinary classroom work. The research to be reported here is therefore distinctive, although not of course unique, in studying teachers at work and in seeking to understand how teachers themselves make sense of the knowledge and thought that they use in their everyday classroom practice. Three practical reasons have been explained for the importance of understanding teachers' professional craft knowledge: the importance in teacher education of enabling beginning teachers to gain access to such knowledge and of enabling experienced teachers to share it with one another; the importance for curricular innovation of understanding the practical knowledge on which teachers depend and which they are therefore typically unwilling to abandon; and the importance for teacher appraisal of knowing how teachers themselves conceptualize and evaluate their teaching, so that any system of appraisal can take full account of this.

2
Identifying 'good teaching'

Different perspectives on good teaching

In the last chapter, we explained how our investigations were designed to concentrate on the elucidation of the professional craft knowledge of teachers and their perceptions of their own teaching. In doing this, however, we had to direct our attention to what in some sense could be identified as 'good teaching' and worthy of emulation. But who is to decide what counts as 'good', and on what basis is that decision made?

There are plenty of people who make judgements on teaching and teachers. Teacher educators decide whether student-teachers are capable of making the transition to become practising teachers. National or state inspectors report officially and publicly on what they observe in classrooms. School principals recommend teachers for promotion. Local district staff pass on information from school to school about the good practice they have seen. Teachers make comments about the capabilities of their colleagues. Parents discuss among themselves the relative merits of different class teachers. Researchers explore the extent to which individual teachers' behaviours fit some theoretical model. Pupils rejoice in evaluating their mentors. And teachers constantly, if unconsciously, assess their own performance.

These groups differ greatly in the extent of their first-hand information about what goes on in classrooms. Parents, principals and teacher colleagues may have only fleeting glimpses of actual teaching in progress. National and local officials often rely on alarmingly small samples of observed practice. Researchers may spend extended periods in classrooms, but they frequently restrict their concerns to highly specific features of the teaching. And teacher educators are exposed to only a narrow window in the teacher's life at a time when the demands, novelty and artificiality of the situation may well produce behaviours which are uncharacteristic of the individual in the longer term. It is only the teachers themselves and their pupils who have comprehensive first-hand knowledge, from their own distinctive perspectives, of what goes on in the classroom.

As well as differing in their opportunities to observe teaching, different groups have different criteria against which they make their judgements about teachers. These have sometimes been concerned with how effectively and efficiently teachers carry out those of their responsibilities which have direct impact on the rest of the school: cooperation with colleagues and the school management, completion of routine administrative duties (records of assessment, registration), organizational competence (extra curricular activities, field trips, parents' evenings), and readiness to react positively to unexpected demands from colleagues, the education system or pupils. In other cases, the criteria have focused on more personal achievements or characteristics, such as:

- How do the teacher's pupils perform in examinations?
- Is this teacher able to keep sufficient control of the class so other teachers remain undisturbed?
- Has he or she managed to complete the course in the time allowed?
- To what extent has this teacher implemented whatever educational innovation is the flavour of the month?
- Does he or she seem to be a warm, encouraging, courteous person with a sense of humour?
- How frequently does this teacher use a particular behaviour (e.g. asks broad questions, responds to pupil initiative, gives pupils feedback) which is hypothesized, by some 'outsider', to lead to a particular kind of learning?

These are but a sample of the plethora of criteria used to judge teaching and teachers. All are salient to some group's concerns for what, in their eyes, constitutes 'good teaching'; but they are of virtually no help to us in our efforts to *understand* teaching. It might seem, therefore, that we had a difficult question to face in deciding how to identify the 'good teaching' on which to focus. In fact, that decision was relatively straightforward for our research in comparison with other kinds.

Selecting good teaching

In the first place, our whole approach was concerned with uncovering the characteristics of the professional craft knowledge which teachers use in their classroom teaching. We could not start, therefore, by claiming that we, or anyone else, knew what it ought to be like. This precluded us from undertaking any kind of 'evaluation' since that would have implied we already had criteria in terms of which to judge the teaching. In no sense was our task one of assessing how far teachers' performances measured up to pre-defined criteria determined by us, school inspectors, principals, parents, colleagues or anyone else. So, unlike evaluators, we were not required to choose among different sets of criteria.

Secondly, we were not aiming to identify effective patterns of teaching in the style of 'process–product' research. That kind of research identifies a particular product of the teaching as evidence of effective teaching. Frequently, that evidence relates to pupil attainment, particularly examination performance. Underlying this approach is the assumption that the teachers' behaviours and the classroom processes are directed towards the achievement of the specified product (e.g. examination results). In our approach, however, we could make no such assumptions about what teachers' activities were directed towards. Furthermore, it was the *teachers'* decision-making with which we were concerned. Patterns of teaching as perceived by an observer who asks how differences in specific teachers' behaviours relate to their achievement of particular products were not what we were looking for. Those patterns would assess the extent to which the observed teaching fitted some outsiders' process–product model, but would tell us little about how the teachers themselves thought about their own classroom activities.

And thirdly, our research could not be planned in relation to any theoretical model of teaching such as inquiry-oriented teaching or mastery learning. Studies which are built around such models must interpret and identify 'good teaching' in ways which reflect the requirements of those theories. But because our purpose was to discover and understand the implicit theories which teachers have and use to guide their own teaching, preconceived theoretical models of teaching could only interfere with the realization of our goal.

It will be clear by this point that our decisions about what was to count as 'good teaching' would depend on judgements made by teachers themselves. The procedure we actually adopted also included judgements made by the other people in the classroom – the pupils.

There were two stages in our selection of 'good teaching':

1 The selection of teachers with whom we would work.
2 The selection of appropriate aspects of those teachers' teaching.

For the first of these, the main criterion we adopted involved asking pupils to describe the strengths of any of their recent teachers. We then looked for consensus among pupils both in their nominations of a particular teacher and about the strengths which were identified for that teacher. Asking pupils to make comments of this kind about their teachers is not, of course, uncontroversial and may, indeed, be seen as threatening by teachers. Anticipating this, we undertook an additional strand in the research in which we explained to teachers what was being asked of pupils, showed them what pupils were saying about their teachers and asked them to think about alternative ways of selecting the teachers with whom we would work.

The second stage in the selection was concerned with choosing the particular aspects of the teaching on which the research would focus. Since a primary aim of the study was to understand the standards (of what is desirable and what is acceptable), which the teacher applies to his or her own teaching and to its effects, it was clear that the choice at this second stage should rest unambiguously with the teacher.

Pupils' perceptions of good teaching: the selection of teachers

The decision to ask pupils to make positive appraisals of their teachers was based on the following four assumptions:

1 Pupils can provide reports of their experiences in classrooms.
2 Their perceptions of those experiences will be related to their own motivations and/or learning.
3 Teaching attempts to influence motivation and learning.
4 There is, therefore, likely to be a connection between what teachers do and pupils' reports of their experiences.

(In interpreting pupils' statements, however, we had to be cautious since they can be influenced by a variety of factors other than their classroom experience.)

The context of the research was mixed ability teaching of the 12 to 14 age group and, to a lesser extent, 10 to 12 year olds. Our work was carried out in one city comprehensive secondary school and four of its 'feeder' primary schools. We found that the 10 year olds represented the lower limit to the age group from which data of this kind could be collected. Our selection of teachers, therefore, was based entirely on statements provided by 12 and 13 year olds.

There were two ways in which we could collect data from pupils about what they thought their teachers did well: they could write down their views or we could interview them (individually or in groups). Since we were interested in the extent to which there was agreement among pupils about the qualities displayed by their teachers, group interviews were inappropriate. In group discussion pupils are likely to be influenced by statements (or known opinions) of their peers; there is a much better chance of eliciting the individual's own views in a private interview or in writing.

Written comments from pupils had the advantage that statements could readily be collected from a large number, agreement (or otherwise) about teachers' qualities could be assessed and the whole procedure could be accomplished in a relatively short time. Among the disadvantages were that we did not know whether pupils would be willing and able to articulate their views on paper, data collected in this way would inevitably be biased towards the statements of the more competent writers and there would be little possibility of probing into what pupils meant by their statements unless the procedure was supplemented by follow-up interviews.

Interviews could have the advantage that pupils are generally able to communicate more fluently by speaking than in writing, and they can be encouraged to elaborate their statements. On the other hand, it is a time-consuming procedure and can have disruptive effects if pupils are extracted individually from class. Furthermore, and like the written mode, it is subject to bias towards the more articulate.

A brief pilot study was undertaken, therefore, to compare the written and oral modes of data collection. At the same time, alternative ways of formulating the task set for the pupils were investigated. In this study, each of four classes of pupils in their second year of secondary school (S2) were asked to think back over their time in that school and to respond to one of the following versions of the question:

- 'Please tell us something about the 3 teachers whose teaching you thought was best. Probably there were different things you liked about each of these teachers. Please say what each teacher did in his or her teaching that you thought was good.'
- 'What do your teachers do well? Tell us which teacher you are talking about and what it is he or she does well.'
- 'What do you think makes a good teacher? Which of your teachers do these things? In each case tell us what he or she does.'
- 'Please tell us about anything you think that any of your teachers do especially well. For each teacher say what it is that he or she does well when teaching.'

The first two versions of the task were most satisfactory for stimulating pupils to focus on the effective teaching qualities of specific teachers, avoiding hypothetical generalities about 'what an ideal teacher would be like' and minimizing emphasis on less relevant characteristics or on negative features (negative statements about teachers, however, were rare). We decided to use the first version of the task for our exploration of pupils' views about their teachers in secondary school, and the following slightly modified version when we asked first-year secondary (S1) pupils to look back to their experience in primary school:

- 'What did your teachers in Primary 6 and Primary 7 do well in their teaching? Probably there were different things you liked about each of these teachers. Please write down each teacher's name and what it was he or she did that was good.'

The investigation of the two modes of response showed us that in the written form, the task elicited plenty of sensible and positive statements from pupils about what their teachers did well. They gave us a wide range of criteria against which they evaluated their teachers, although the detail provided was limited. The constructs they used were expressed in brief statements ('She helps you when you're stuck', 'He explains so you understand') without elaboration of *how* their teachers did the things they did well. The actual collection of the data was straightforward. After an initial introduction to the task from the researchers (in the absence of any teacher) the pupils fussed around for about 10 minutes, asked a series of questions (which expressed some astonishment at what they were being asked to do) and then settled down to complete their sheets. Almost all pupils wrote several distinctive statements about several teachers.

In the oral form, the interviewer was able to use non-directive probing to persuade pupils to clarify and elaborate to some extent on the brief statements they made about their teachers' strengths. This was achieved, however, only in circumstances where they had *already completed the written task*. Without that, when faced with the unfamiliar question in a one-to-one interview their reaction was to claim they had nothing to say. They really needed the 10 minutes which they had in the written mode to collect their thoughts and re-orient themselves; in an interview, however, even a 10 second pause can seem an eternity. Our conclusion from this was that within our resources the only feasible way to proceed was to use the written mode.

We have collected many hundreds of statements from pupils about what their teachers do well. These have seemed to us overwhelmingly appropriate and discerning. The ways in which pupils responded to the task in reasonable and constructive ways was encouraging, and they showed a considerable appreciation of what their teachers were trying to do. We are not suggesting, of course, that the statements offered a prescription for teaching, and one of our primary concerns had to be with teachers' reactions to the idea of us collecting these kinds of data from pupils. We speculated that they might:

- Feel threatened by the stockpiling of pupils' comments (albeit favourable) about their teaching.
- Distrust pupils' ability to evaluate teaching properly.
- Be apprehensive about the effect of the task on teacher–pupil relationships.
- Be afraid that 'discipline might suffer irrevocably if children are publicly permitted to flex their critical muscles'.

(Wragg and Wood 1984: 79)

The whole staff (57) of the comprehensive school was asked, therefore, to scrutinize the (anonymized) statements from 75 S2 pupils. These pupils had identified 44 teachers in 18 subject areas who had taught them at some time during the two years as displaying positive qualities in the classroom. The teachers' reactions to the statements suggested that most of their original fears of the procedure had diminished. They found the statements interesting and, in some cases, of value; they recollected making similar judgements in their own school days; and they commented that pupils are the 'customers' of education and for this reason alone note must be taken of their comments. There seemed little disagreement with the view that the pupils' statements were in no sense inflammatory. On the contrary, they were seen as 'predictable', 'nothing new', 'nothing more than common sense', 'fairly obvious' and 'just concerned with what we are supposed to be doing anyway'.

At this stage the teachers were reacting to the 'raw data' of pupils' statements. It was clear, however, that at various stages during the research the statements would have to be categorized in some way. We did not believe that it would be feasible, in practice, for us to involve pupils themselves in the categorization process (in theory such a procedure should be followed if valid groupings are to be made). It seemed inevitable that we, as researchers, would have to be responsible for formulating the categories despite this apparently undermining the emphasis which this project puts on teachers' and pupils' (rather than outsiders') constructs of effective teaching. It was possible, however, to ask teachers to engage at this stage in the research in a process of thinking about how pupils' statements might be grouped together in categories. Their categories could then be compared with those generated independently by us and, if no great differences were found, we could have greater confidence in our own grouping of statements throughout the rest of the project.

Our own categorization (not revealed to the teachers) grouped the statements from these S2 pupils under 10 headings as shown in Table 2.1. Apart from the last one, each heading reflects some imagined aspect of a teacher's intentions. The examples are verbatim statements written by pupils.

It must be emphasized that these categories do not describe any individual teacher's qualities. They reflect the statements of one group of pupils about their teachers. Different pupils or a different stage in schooling might produce quite different categories, and teachers might well have categorized the statements in ways other than ours. We put the teachers' categorization to the test by asking the school's 57 staff members, in groups of about 10 individuals, to scrutinize a random sample of 60 of the pupils' statements. There was a high consensus among the groups in the ways in which they saw the statements as naturally grouping together to form categories. Furthermore, the eight categories which they identified had a

Table 2.1 What is it that pupils say their teachers do well?

Category 1: *Creation of a relaxed and enjoyable atmosphere in the classroom*
e.g. 'He is a bit strickt but he tryes to crack jokes when he can.'
'She never moans a lot and is a good laugh.'
'He is a teacher that teases people nicely and they can do it back to him.'

Category 2: *Retention of control in the classroom*
e.g. 'He is good at controling the class, dosnt shout alot.'
'She doesn't have to keep telling you to sit down and be quiet.'
'She is good at keeping her cool when people are misbehaving.'

Category 3: *Presentation of work in a way which interests and motivates pupils*
e.g. 'He don't make it boring in the classroom it is not solid working through the whole period.'
'She is good at making stories funny and interesting.'
'He tries to vary our work by doing one thing one day and another thing the next.'

Category 4: *Providing conditions so pupils understand the work*
e.g. 'She is good at explaining things to you.'
'You can understand what he is saying.'
'He told us and demonstrated so we understood.'

Category 5: *Making clear what pupils are to do and achieve*
e.g. 'She explains what we are to do in detail.'
'I think the things he is good at is explaining what you have to do.'
'He makes sure we understand what we have to do.'

Category 6: *Judging what can be expected of a pupil*
e.g. 'She lets you do your work in your own time.'
'He doesn't give you too much work.'
'She doesnt make you work too fast and get mad when you do something wrong!'

Category 7: *Helping pupils with difficulties*
e.g. 'He helps you every time you are stuck and is patient.'
'If you cant do something he will spend time with you might not learn how to do it but at least you'll be able to say you've improved.'
'She understands the problems you have in class and helps with the questions.'

Category 8: *Encouragement of pupils to raise their expectations of themselves*
e.g. 'He helps pupils who aren't very good at it to have confidence in themselves.'
'He gives you encouragement and has taught us to give others encouragement'.
'She makes you believe you can do more.'

Table 2.1 (Cont.)

Category 9:	*Development of personal, mature relationships with pupils*
e.g.	'I like her because of her understanding and the way she treated you like a 14 year old and not a 9 year old.'
	'She understands young people and gives you help when you need it.'
	'She is a very good teacher to talk to.'
Category 10:	*Teacher's personal talents (subject-related or other)*
e.g.	'At maths he really knows what he's talking about.'
	'She is very good at art herself.'
	'He's great at Karate.'

close correspondence with categories 1, 2, 3, 4, 6, 7, 9 and 10 which we had formulated. When the sample of 60 statements was examined it was found that by chance it included only one statement in each of the researchers' categories 5 and 8. It was not surprising, therefore, that the teachers had not identified this pair of groupings.

The similarities between the ways in which we and the teachers had chosen to group the pupils' statements were encouraging. It suggested that the distinctions which we as researchers would have to make, among the different things which teachers are seen as doing well, would make sense to, and be seen as sensible by, teachers themselves. There was, however, a note of caution to be sounded. In two of the categories, 'Creation of a relaxed and enjoyable atmosphere in the classroom' and 'Judging what can be expected of a pupil', the pupils' statements were valued by the researchers differently from some of the teachers. We had a 'positive' view of both groups of statements. In contrast, a minority of the teachers suggested that the first of these categories implied a classroom characterized by entertainment, amusement, encouragement of pupils to have 'a carry on' and not offering what they would regard as acceptable evidence of good teaching. And statements in the second of these categories were interpreted by a few teachers as evidence that pupils were not being pushed hard enough and 'slackers' were being encouraged. As time went on and we collected more statements, we were inclined to think the teachers were right about the second of these categories, but not the first.

From the pupils, then, we had clear pointers to where they thought we would find aspects of good teaching. And we had some confidence that the teachers felt more comfortable than they had expected to be about the majority of the pupils' criteria for 'good teaching'. That tentative acceptance was expressed by one teacher in the following way:

You try to motivate them, keep them interested, be understanding, don't go off the deep end. If that is what I thought I should be doing in the classroom, and now the kids are saying that, the two things come together and . . . what they're saying could be a method of choosing teachers.

Most of the teachers, however, felt that pupils' statements were not a *sufficient* basis for selection. The problem they then faced was to suggest ways in which these commentaries from the 'consumers' of teaching could be supplemented. One supplementary procedure, which gained universal support, and which we subsequently implemented, required that individual teachers should be given the opportunity to recognize and assent or dissent from the positive statements made about them by their pupils. Beyond that, various ideas for other means of selecting teachers were made, but all were greeted with substantial reservations by other teachers. For example, it was suggested that

- Selection be based on national examination results for pupils of age 16 or older; but would that have relevance for the qualities displayed by the teacher in mixed ability classes for 10 to 14 year olds?
- A random sample of teachers be taken; but would that give an adequate spread across subjects or across the range of things which teachers do well?
- We should call for volunteers and make no effort to approach other teachers; but is that the best way to get at teachers who do particular things well?
- Members of staff should be asked to nominate colleagues; but teachers seldom see each other teaching so how would they decide who to recommend?
- One very experienced, one moderately experienced and one inexperienced teacher should be selected; but is experience the most salient factor in what the research is looking for?
- A class of older pupils should be asked first to estimate what their teachers are trying to do and then to make statements about what they are doing well; but is that an appropriate way to identify what teachers do well with classes of younger pupils?
- Video recordings of lessons should be made; but how does one decide who to video-record, and who makes the judgements based on the videos?

In the end, the teachers agreed that despite their desire to add something to pupils' statements as a means of selection, they could think of no satisfactory procedure.

In selecting the teachers with whom we would like to work, however, it was not enough simply to choose those who were mentioned by a substantial number of pupils and about whom there was a measure of agreement on their particular strengths. In addition, we sought a sample of teachers who would display a variety of qualities and whose specialisms represented a number of different areas of the school curriculum. On this basis, we identified 28 teachers with whom we felt it would be valuable to work. The availability and willingness of these teachers and the time at our disposal reduced this number to 16. Four were primary teachers and 12 secondary with subject specialisms in art, computing, English (two), French, geography, history, outdoor education, physical education, mathematics and science (two).

It is clear that our sample of teachers was biased. We selected them on the basis of their pupils' perceptions of their strengths, and we undoubtedly worked with a group of people who had particularly good relationships with their pupils. Had we used other criteria for our selection (e.g. the recommendations of inspectors or of principals, examination results, nominations by colleagues, volunteers), we would almost certainly not have ended up with an identical sample. A second point to be made is that our small cross-curricular sample will not allow us to explain any differences observed between teachers as differences between their respective subject areas. With only one or two teachers in each specialism we cannot partial out the effect of the subject from that of the individual teacher. On the other hand, however, any generalizations we can make across this sample will be the more powerful because of the diversity of specialisms.

Teachers' self-evaluation

Having used the pupils' views to select teachers, we then looked to the teachers to select the aspects of their teaching to which our attention would be directed. In our initial approach, each of the 16 teachers was given a summary of the statements made about him or her by the pupils. This provided very considerable positive reinforcement. Teachers seldom have the opportunity to read such encouraging feedback about their own performance. The pupils' recognition and appreciation of what their teachers were trying to do for (and with) them came as a pleasant surprise, and made the researcher's job much easier thereafter.

Negotiations were then carried out with each teacher and all agreed to work with us on a 'unit of work' (or part of such a unit) of their own choice. This unit encompassed between two and six hours of teaching. While the concept of a 'unit of work' sounds neat, in practice it meant many different things. With the primary teachers it was interpreted as two mornings' work including language, number work, projects, reading, stories, science, television programmes and so on. In the secondary school it meant a set of art lessons devoted to making masks, part of the work on a play ('Johnny Salter'), a section in a French course ('Circuite Touristique' in *Tour de France*), the properties of rectangles, a series of fairly self-contained lessons in computing, a set of topics in geography using maps, a number of periods of basketball, an outdoor education expedition to a river gorge, part of the work on a story ('A Pair of Jesus Boots'), two different sections of a resource-based science course ('The Plant and Animal Kingdoms' and 'Cells') and a section of a history course ('The Romans').

Each 'unit of work' was directly observed by a researcher and all of the teacher's talk was recorded on audio-tape. At the end of each lesson (or, in the case of the primary teachers, in the middle and at the end of each morning) the teachers were asked to tell us about *those aspects of their teaching which had particularly pleased them, they felt they had done well or had given them satisfaction*.

These accounts by the teachers provided the core of the research data. They gave us a means of identifying the criteria which teachers use to evaluate their own 'good teaching', and of understanding something of how they construe their classroom practice.

In the next chapter, we look first at how we collected from the teachers the information about what they valued, and found to work well, in their own teaching. Secondly, we examine in some detail how the teachers talked about their good teaching.

Summary

In this chapter we have discussed the problem of identifying 'good teaching' and have explained how we tackled it. We have discussed the different groups accustomed to evaluating teachers, the varying degrees to which such evaluations are informed, and the diversity of criteria likely to be used; and we have discussed too the implications of our distinctive purpose in seeking to understand teachers' professional craft knowledge. We have described the procedure adopted, which depended in the first instance on the comments of individual pupils about what they liked about the teaching of those teachers who they thought were the best of those they had experienced during the previous two years. A pilot study gave us confidence in the feasibility of obtaining appropriate written comments from pupils in their early secondary school years, comments covering many aspects of teaching. A further study sought the reactions of teachers in the secondary comprehensive school in which most of the main investigation was to be conducted. The teachers found the pupils' comments unexceptional and 'fairly obvious', and they categorized these comments in much the same way as the researchers had, although not all teachers valued everything that pupils had admired. No alternative approaches to teacher selection commanded general approval among the teachers. Twenty-eight teachers were selected on the basis of some consensus about their strengths, and in order to represent a variety of qualities and a range of subject specialisms. Sixteen of these who were willing and available participated in the main investigation, including four primary teachers and representing among the others a range of secondary specialisms. Each was initially given a summary of pupil comments, and each identified a 'unit of work' to be observed by a researcher and recorded, with the teachers reporting at the end of each lesson those aspects of their teaching which had particularly pleased them.

3

How do teachers talk about their good teaching?

Problems of making the familiar explicit

To be asked to talk about the ordinary, everyday, familiar things one does spontaneously, routinely, habitually in the classrooms, is to be presented with a very difficult task. The things which are done automatically, even unconsciously, are the hardest to articulate and, in normal circumstances, teachers are rarely required to make them explicit.

At the start, we did not know whether teachers would be able to tell us about their classroom teaching. Could we be confident that they would understand what kind of information we were seeking from them? Could we make clear to them that we were interested in the criteria *they* used in making their own judgements about situations, and in their own decision-making and action taking? Could we persuade them that we were not interested in imported theories about what they, as teachers, ought to be doing? Could we assume that the information we sought would even be available to teachers? Could they bring to their consciousness the mental processes they engage in subconsciously during their teaching? Could we dissuade them from inventing answers for us? If the information was available, could we motivate them to give it to us? If they gave it to us, could we check its validity?

What we were asking of teachers was something which they were unaccustomed to doing and would be likely to find difficult. There were few obvious rewards in it for them, so why should they make the effort to help us? It was imperative that we should adopt a strategy which, as far as possible, would meet and deal with the various problems we envisaged.

A strategy for collecting information

To achieve this, one major strand of our strategy was to make clear to teachers that we were taking a *positive* perspective on teaching. We explained to each teacher how he or she came to be invited to participate, gave them summaries of the comments their pupils had made about their strengths, and emphasized that we believed these strengths were worthy of elucidation and explanation. The teachers seemed unaccustomed to attention being focused on their strengths rather than their weaknesses, and they appreciated the new emphasis. They were also unused to receiving systematic feedback on what their pupils admired in them. This approach appeared to have a motivating effect and to engender confidence in the teachers to talk about and explain their actions in the classroom.

The positive perspective was maintained when we went into the teachers' classrooms. Throughout the observed unit of work, opportunities were taken at the end of each lesson (or part of a morning in a primary school) to ask the teachers to say as much as they could about what had gone well and what they had valued in their own teaching on that occasion. The pupils were also asked to express their views by writing down what they thought the teacher had done well. Their comments seemed sensible and appropriate. For example:

- 'She spent time explaining what to do. She explains everything not just says "do this, do that".'
- 'And he helps you if you are stuck or if you did something wrong.'
- 'She spoke loud and clear. And didn't lecture us and let us take a part in asking and answering questions.'
- 'He has a good sense of humour. The play and the voices and the way he joins in. He is quite a character.'

These were made available in anonymized form to the teachers a few days later. Once again, the statements seemed to have a pleasurable and motivating effect, even if some teachers tried not to let this be too apparent.

A second important strand of the research strategy ensured that all the data we collected (from interviews with teachers, statements made by pupils and observations by researchers) referred to the same set of *shared experiences*. The main reason for the researcher's observation of the lessons, and one reason for the recording of them, was to give both the teacher and researcher a specific set of teaching events which they could discuss. The questions asked, prompts given and the information collected about the pupils' perspectives on the events, were all concerned with those shared experiences in the classroom. The emphasis on such experiences had three effects:

1 It reinforced the point that the focus of the research was on what actually happens in classrooms.
2 It constrained the teachers to concentrate on real and shared events rather than imagined reconstructions.
3 It provided the means for a limited check, from the researchers' observations and the audio recording, on the teachers' accounts of what had happened.

The third crucial strand of our strategy relates to our efforts to maintain, and be seen to maintain, a very *open approach*. Everything was done to avoid the imposition of any of our preconceptions of how teaching should be construed or evaluated, and of the relationships which do or should arise between teachers' activities and those of pupils. It was made clear that the researchers wanted to understand what pleased the teachers about the observed lessons. Even when prompts were introduced into the interviews, these were from the lessons themselves, from what the teacher had said, or from pupils' comments, and *not* from the researcher's ideas. Openness on our part was seen as essential if the teachers were to be encouraged to bring to consciousness their own perceptions, concepts and decision-making processes. We had to avoid circumstances which would encourage them to fit their responses to our questions into frameworks offered by *us*. It was important to heed warnings of what McNamara (1980) calls 'The Outsider's Arrogance' and to follow Spradley's (1979: 11) advice: 'Before you impose your theories on the people you study, find out how these people define the world'.

The fourth strand of our approach was concerned with our efforts to *help the teachers to gain access to the information* we were seeking. The interviews were designed to make it as easy as possible for teachers to recall their experience of the lessons and to identify and explain what was involved in those aspects of the lessons which they saw as the most successful. A most important feature of the interviews was that they were undertaken as soon as possible after the lesson, preferably immediately and certainly the same day. This ensured that the events were still fresh in everyone's minds.

We experimented with written statements from the teachers but, unlike our experience with the pupils, the oral form of communication turned out to be more satisfactory. In the first place the teachers voiced a preference for offering their views orally; they could express themselves more readily, felt supported by the interviewer and were able to get more information across in the relatively brief time available at the end of the lesson. A second reason concerned the substance, and relative value to the research, of the responses in the two modes. Understandably, the written responses were brief, sometimes at a high level of generality and somewhat staccato in form. When asked to give oral accounts, however, the teachers spoke more expansively, often referred to classroom events in concrete terms, and were more likely to describe what they did and why.

> Steven's, I knew, wasn't going to be particularly good but he I hope would be pleased that his work was shown to the rest of the class, although you might have noticed that I didn't in fact hold the thing up . . . because it was scrawled, it wasn't very good but he had the three main points which he was told to put in . . . and I looked at it and said 'Yes, you've got the three main points. Well done, Steven!' and put it back. So that's just encouragement.

The oral accounts, therefore, were easier to interpret, provided more detailed information about the teachers' evaluations of themselves and were likely to offer insight into their perceptions of their own teaching. The more complete picture offered by the spoken word in comparison with the written reports also helped us to identify commonalities and significant differences among the teachers. The more abbreviated written responses found the teachers describing their own strengths within differing and rather limited frameworks. Thus, one teacher would write mainly in terms of what the pupils did in the lesson, without identifying what teacher activity promoted the desired pupil behaviour; another might refer to a teacher behaviour but omit identification of its effect on the pupils; while a third might mention pupil achievements, without reference to either the pupil or teacher activity which preceded the achievement.

In addition to the collection of their accounts immediately after the lessons, the teachers were given the chance to reflect on the classroom events and express their views a second time. Each was given audio-tapes of the recorded lessons and interviewed some two weeks later. The same general question was asked inquiring about what they thought had been good about their teaching, and giving them the opportunity, having listened to the tapes, to make other comments and to elaborate on what they had said before. Interestingly, very few new themes were identified. Sometimes matters which had been referred to immediately after the lesson were taken up once more and spoken about at greater length. There was also a tendency for the teachers to alight upon what they saw as negative features, such as voice characteristics or mannerisms, which were accentuated by the recording but not a concern of the research.

As with the earlier interviews, the researcher refrained from making any substantive contribution to the discussion of what had gone well in the lessons. Apart from the opening question, the researcher's role was primarily one of probing and prompting: 'Can you explain that a little more?', 'Is there anything else you would like to say?', 'Can you give me more detail?', 'Are there other things you thought were good about your teaching?', 'What was it about that that was good?', 'How did you achieve that?'.

We did conduct, however, one further interview with each teacher in which we used various tactics to facilitate their recall. Having identified themes in the teachers' earlier conversations with us, we asked them to elaborate on what they had already said. To help them in this, they were shown relevant pupils' comments and played appropriate extracts from the lessons. In this way, they were stimulated to explicate further the nature and detail of the themes. We were aware, of course, that the data collected in this phase of the work may have been subject to some contamination from the researcher. In selecting themes, pupils' statements, teachers' statements and lesson extracts, for the purpose of encouraging the teachers to clarify and elaborate further the various strengths they perceived in their own teaching, it is possible that the researchers' interpretations of what was going on in the lessons had some impact on what the teachers said. We tried to minimize this as much as we could, and where we had any doubts the data collected in this part of the work were not used in the analysis.

It was clear from the start that the teachers with whom we worked reflected a wide variety of characteristics which, it might be guessed, could influence their approaches to teaching. There were primary and secondary teachers, men (seven, two of whom were primary) and women (nine, two of whom were primary), representatives from 10 secondary specialisms, individuals whose style could be judged 'traditional' and those identified as 'progressive' and a range of age from the 20s to the 60s. How do the members of such a 'mixed bag' talk about their teaching? What are the criteria they use in evaluating their own performances? In what ways do they differ from each other in the way they talk and what they talk about?

The different things which teachers value in their teaching

Our considerable efforts to adopt open interviewing procedures were rewarded by an extensive, rich, complex and varied set of data from all the teachers. Only one teacher tried to persuade us to 'lead me into it' by asking her specific questions, and she laughed as she made her request. These data made it possible to reconstruct detailed descriptions derived from the 12 secondary and four primary teachers' 'inside' accounts of what goes on in their classrooms. Even a casual glance made it clear that there was considerable variation among the teachers both in what they identified as having pleased them about their teaching and in the ways they talked about these things.

We found we were able to identify for each individual a small number of 'themes' which they brought into their accounts of their lessons. As we shall see, these themes confirmed that the teachers involved in this research were not out on some esoteric limb. Their concerns mirror much of what has been said and written about 'good teaching' over the centuries.

We also found substantial variation among the teachers in how they talked about their teaching. Some concentrated on what happened in the observed lessons, others talked primarily about the general strategies which they habitually used in their teaching. Some focused, as asked, on what they were pleased with while others tended to drift towards the things they were unhappy about. Some talked overwhelmingly about their pupils, others said more about their own activities. And these were not the only ways in which teachers' accounts differed from one another. The richness of their diversity engendered in us both a warm feeling about variety in classrooms and also mild terror about the task of achieving a coherent analysis of this collection of data.

In Chapters 4 and 5 we will be analysing in some depth the structure of the teachers' accounts, and providing extensive illustration of the concepts they used in talking about their teaching. In this chapter, however, our aim is to provide a general flavour of the themes they used in describing and evaluating what they had been doing. Those themes covered a wide range of different aspects of teaching, including:

- How they maintain the interest and enthusiasm of their pupils.
- How they diffuse actual or potential discipline problems.
- How their planning interacts with their management of classes and of lessons.
- Their approaches to taking account of the characteristics of individual pupils.
- The ways in which they deal with pupils' errors.
- Their attempts to build up confidence and trust with pupils.
- How they manage their introductions to the lessons.
- Their provision of clear explanations so pupils understand the work.
- How they provide help for pupils.
- How they manage question and answer sessions.

The rest of this chapter illustrates the ways in which some of the teachers talked about the first three of these themes. Our intention is to provide a taste of how individuals go about discussing their teaching, and to give some sense of the diversity and texture of their accounts.

Pupils' interest and enthusiasm

One major preoccupation of many of the teachers was the importance of maintaining the interest and enthusiasm of the pupils. While a few of the views expressed on how to sustain interest were common across teachers (e.g. 'A wee bit of variation as far as the teacher's concerned', 'Not sticking to the same thing for 20 minutes. Then it can be really boring'), most of the statements seemed to be context specific.

In some cases, a 'performance' on the part of the teacher can be a most effective way of capturing, or recapturing, pupils' interest. We encountered one example of a splendid piece of acting by a secondary English teacher when he suddenly took part in a play reading. The pupils' performance and the audience's attention had patently degenerated over the lesson, but his intervention changed things dramatically for the better. In his description of the event he said:

> In the hope of generating either response or some interest from them, I asked what they thought of the play. It wasn't very compli- mentary . . . One has to think very quickly what you're going to do about getting yourself out of the hole which you've got yourself into . . . with something like another 40 minutes to go . . . One cannot suddenly say 'Right, we'll stop reading. Get your books out, we'll do some written work' because that compounds the felony. So my only solution . . . was to go into the play further. I took a part myself, and I tried to speed the thing up, regenerate the play . . . They were quite interested in the fight, but that's only because it was being spoken through by me, I was able to keep it going. The main thing is the reading, and their's was pathetic.

This teacher, however, was conscious of the complexity of the situation. He observed that while it might be thought that interest could be better sustained if the play was cast so as to include only those who would pro- duce competent performances, this approach would be a non-starter because (in his view) the teacher must aim to give everyone in the class a chance to participate. This exemplified a conflict of goals for him, and we were repeatedly to come across such conflict as our work progressed.

A teacher of French also used the tactic of interjecting some drama into the classroom discourse by using different voices in reading a text:

> I think it worked, doing the change in voices so that it's not just the boring same level of intonation all the way along. If they know if it's a woman or a man or it's an official voice, providing they don't go too far, that helps to keep the interest. I like doing that and they like doing it. You have to be lively yourself as well . . . If I'm just standing there, repeating in a monotone, then I can't expect them to be any- thing else . . . that can just turn them off completely.

In another subject area, computing studies, the teacher saw the pupils' enthusiasm as being dependent on the intrinsic interest of the various activities which they were expected to undertake in the course of a lesson:

> Something that bores them to tears is straightforward jotter work where they are having to answer question after question. They are interested in *doing*, or maybe interested in *learning about*, but not

straightforward *writing* . . . they are psyched up, they want to get on to the machines.

The art teacher saw the maintenance of the level of enthusiasm as a process of selecting inherently interesting tasks and then 'keeping the momentum going and keeping them working for as much of the time as possible'. In describing how she facilitated their imaginative work she said:

I was trying to get the imaginations going as well as the straight-forward skills of drawing. When I was going round the class I was keeping things going and helping . . . so they didn't get stuck on the *technical* problems and then lose interest . . . They could keep their enthusiasm going saying 'Oh I want it to be like such-and-such. I want horns like this or like that'. Now up to a point I want *them* to draw the horns like that, but if they've shown me in their original drawing that . . . they've tried but they're just having problems getting it as they want, then if it's a pupil that I think if I say 'Go away and do it yourself' that they'll then become discouraged and feel they can't do it as they really want and, therefore, there's no point in doing it at all, then I think it's better for me to give them some help . . . It's a prob-lem in art just knowing how much to do for them. There's no point in them just colouring in what I've drawn for them . . . When it's genu-inely someone who is concerned, wants to get on, is stuck, lacks confidence, then if it takes just a couple of wee strokes with a pencil and a few words here and there, then I'd rather do that.

The outdoor education teacher described a strategy he uses all the time to prevent boredom and anticlimax, and to bring out the pupils' excitement and interest through discovery:

I do try to make the castle a discovery rather than a presentation . . . more of an adventure as in a sort of story, rather than being in a park where everything's laid out . . . The castle as a whole does tend to reveal itself stage by stage . . . climbing up to it you only see the ruin of the wall, then through it you're into the courtyard, and then the bridge and the sudden big drop, and they still don't realize that it's four storeys down until they go round the back and they suddenly realize that they've been away up in the air . . . If they see too much at once . . . they wouldn't be able to just concentrate on each bit at a time, whereas it does make an impression if they're discovering as they go round it.

How the teachers recognized when pupils were interested was not altogether clear. It seemed that lack of negative indicators were the cues they looked for most often.

- 'I didn't hear many groans at the start of the period.'
- 'When they came in there were no grumbles.'
- 'If they pay less attention to what's going on around them and more attention to what they're doing . . . the fact that they're not always turning round.'

Maintaining discipline

None of the lessons we observed displayed any obvious discipline problems. There were visible differences, however, among the teachers in the extent to which they found certain behaviours, such as chat among pupils or pupils moving independently around the room, acceptable. The sample of teachers, of course, had been selected in a way which ensured that some aspects at least of their teaching were appreciated by the pupils; and the pupils had firmly stated to us that they liked well-ordered if relaxed teaching.

What became clear as the research progressed, however, was that disciplined activity was not maintained just by chance or through force of teacher personality. These teachers worked hard and constantly at creating order and sustaining good working relationships with their pupils. They had developed a variety of tactics and strategies which seemed to work for them, and which we will exemplify here.

At the tactical level, teachers frequently mentioned how important it was to be prepared to stop talking, to pause and to 'look' at pupils to bring them to order. One of the primary teachers, however, discussed the need to conclude such episodes on a friendly and positive note:

> They're not bad . . . You need the 'word' here and there and the 'look'. I 'looked' a lot. That won't come over on the tape but I did; I look, I stare, and sometimes, depending on the child, it works actually if you just then sometimes *smile* at them. They sort of 'Oh, she's looking', appeal to their better nature if they've got any . . . It really does, rather than be sour or a reprimand, if you just smile it sometimes works.'

Another teacher valued the calmness of his approach. His aim was to establish and maintain a steady, disciplined unruffled routine in his resource-based science class:

> I try to have this effect of calming things by non-reacting and just by speaking in a kind of subdued way . . . I listened to both tapes and what struck me was the way that nothing seemed to cause me to panic at any time. There's just a very, very steady delivery so no matter what the children thought was a serious problem . . . it didn't

produce in me any kind of hysteria . . . a soothing presence . . . sort of envelop them in a kind of snoozy equality, so that nothing seemed to escalate.

Occasionally teachers provided very full accounts of strategies they had developed. In particular, the computing studies teacher comprehensively described the measures he took to deal with recalcitrant pupils, and the importance he placed on maintaining good relations with them, despite their misbehaviour. He was convinced that a crucial element in a strategy of this kind concerns the teacher dealing with the problem in ways which prevent the pupil becoming alienated from the work:

I think [it's wise to use] quite a good mixture of the possible ways to deal with . . . pupils who, you know, don't behave in the way you would like them to . . . What I've used with Thomas is the threat of overtime, staying behind the rest to finish off the work which means that he might work a wee bit harder and by working harder he will have less time to, you know, cause problems. There's straightforward telling off . . . I don't use it a lot because I think it affects the rest of the class . . . It was a different way of handling Thomas in which I asked him a question . . . He was involved in disrupting another pupil at the time, and to draw his attention to the lesson and draw everybody else's attention I asked him the answer to a question and I kept his attention while I checked out on the board. And then at the end of checking it out I congratulated him on getting it right so that maybe gave him something to look forward to in the next question. So that was a wee bit of positive reinforcement.

We were working towards repairing the rift that already happened . . . You know, after I've told him that he's to stay behind . . . he's probably, you know, starting to think of ways he can disrupt the lesson . . . so I've got to think of things to repair our feelings towards each other . . . I don't want to give him a punishment at the end of the lesson, I want to try and get my way of thinking over to him . . . that, you know, the only person who's going to suffer is himself . . . if you can give him some encouragement through the work that he's done, then you're on a winning streak.

We saw the same with Craig, the new boy. I had to move his seat, but I didn't just move him and leave him. I found it beneficial to go across and spend quite a bit of time with him and, you know, trying to work up a relationship before I had to give him a further reprimand . . . if you're going to make these reprimands or the corrective action work, then you've got to have some sort of relationship between pupil and teacher. You find that most pupils . . . will not accept reprimands from people they don't know . . . that's why it's a lot easier once you've been in a school for a year, because people know you . . . it really hurts them if they get a reprimand from, you know, a teacher who's one of their friends as it were . . . But you've got to go about it the right way. Don't work at getting the children to like you. The children will like you if you go about, you know, your business in the normal way.

Maintaining discipline is clearly a context specific matter. It depends on what counts as a well-ordered or disciplined classroom for the individual teacher. It is influenced by the circumstances in which the teaching is carried out; the particular group of pupils, the time of day and the material environment can all affect the standards which can be sustained. And finally, teachers take those actions which they find work best for them in achieving their discipline goals; different teachers may share some of the same preferences for action, but they also display considerable individual variation.

Plans and management

Because our study was directed towards what actually goes on in classrooms, we did not expect teachers to talk much about the planning of their teaching. As it turned out, however, several teachers initiated discussions about their general approaches to planning and the ways in which it interacts with their management of the classroom work. What made this particularly interesting was that they did not treat planning as a specific aspect of their work distinct from, for example, classroom teaching or evaluation. They tended to have some basic, consistent, planned pattern for their teaching, but this pattern was always flexible and influenced by the circumstances of the lesson itself. It was clear that they set up broad and pre-planned frameworks to guide the teaching and learning, but the conditions which impinged on the teaching on any particular occasion would affect the actions taken by the teacher and so the detail of the implementation of their plans. In many cases it appeared that the teachers' aim was to establish a pattern of working that was consistent from lesson to lesson and which pupils would come to take for granted on every occasion.

For example, one primary teacher described his approach to the management of the different aspects of work for each member of his class (his class was a composite of sixth and seventh year primary children). He appeared to have a clearly planned strategy which he saw as achieving particular goals for his pupils, especially that of fostering positive attitudes towards school. In the following excerpt, he describes what he saw as his informal plan for organizing the work for the day, and he comments on how he took specific action to suit pupils who are not predisposed to fit in with his approach:

It strikes me that you may have considered my start to the day as terribly informal, there's no 'good morning', they don't have to stand up, we've no lining up . . . I want them to be organizing their own day . . . They have the responsibility of making sure they get their work covered . . . If they've finished the work they can go and put a [computer] program on, they can play chess, scrabble, things like that all with educational content. So there I was just basically going over each one's plan for the morning to remind everybody what I'd like covered . . . The little boy, John, there are children like that who, when they've finished a specific task, or they *know* they've got their spelling, and they *know* they've got their mental, and then they're waiting on *me* to teach maths, he would sit and do nothing . . . used to being guided through every moment of the day . . . I tell them they can cope, mark all their own maths, for instance, I trust them . . . Children who cheat, we talk it over, I give them a row, try to get them not to do it again. So they're going to have far more say in their education . . . I hope they say 'I want to go in to school today because I've got a game of chess to finish' . . . or 'it's my turn to go on the computer if I get my work done' . . . I'm reminding those children who need it what's to be done in the gaps between formal education . . . To me it's not a *formal* plan.

Another teacher, of secondary science in a resource-based scheme, described how her plan for managing the work of the class was based on the importance of pupils taking responsibility for following a systematic sequence of procedures in the laboratory. In the following statements she identifies the 'routine' she had planned and how she set about achieving it; she makes it clear that this was a long-term undertaking:

It's essential to have a *routine* to start with. I would hope that my classes could come in and be taken by anyone and still do the same work in the same way . . . It's built up over a long time, some get it right quickly, other classes you struggle away at it. I like them to come in in a certain way, hang up their coats, put their bags under their coat rack. I prefer them to sit at the front when they're writing and move to the back only when they're doing experiments. When they come in they get a lot of safety rules, but you impose . . . your own routine on that . . . The procedure for going to [the technician] to borrow equipment, getting their rough books checked, it's all hard work and repeating yourself for about the first month . . . Things like, I won't let them go until everyone's quiet and they're all standing ready to go and then I let them go, one line at a time. And it's important to do that to keep them under control, because in this situation you don't have 'sit down, keep quiet', it's just not that at all.

It's all built up, you know, one day after another. You're on the horns of a dilemma because you want them to get in and do the experiments, but they've got to know the way to do them and you don't want to start off with a big long list 'you must do this, you must do that' . . . Or when a new thing comes up when they have to collect something from [the technician], then I would stop the class and say 'Look, this worksheet says you've got to collect something . . . and the procedure for that is that you're polite, number one, and you ask nicely for things and you read the sheet and you make sure you know exactly what you're asking for' . . . But you can't do it all at once.

A major concern for a teacher of mathematics was the management of time. She was conscious of how her decisions on the pacing of the lesson, and on the apportioning of time among the different activities, was influenced by the conditions or circumstances of the teaching (e.g. time of day, duration of lesson, content):

Time of day is quite crucial, I mean ideally they should come in the morning, but they don't, timetabling constraints . . . afternoons it's quite often better if they are restless to have a 10 minute session of me explaining things at the beginning that seems to settle them, but I know how long I want to teach for and how much I must cover, 10 to 15 minutes is about it. In the afternoon they're less able to keep their heads down and to keep on.

In a single period there never is time, but in a double period about three-quarters of the way through they're restless, they will try for a short time but the spells get shorter and shorter and I have to adjust.

This time I've given them a list of properties [on the blackboard] and shown them how they actually work by turning the shapes round, but this is a *specific* unit, it's a *lot* of class teaching with this one. Most of the others are nothing like that . . . maybe a short 5 minutes of this, 10 minutes going over something they might meet, then give problems and they come and get the stuff corrected.

I try and set a *type* of lesson plan down . . . a deliberate pattern . . . then that's the way I'd do the next one with the other shapes. They [the pupils] get to know it . . . but you have to vary it.

In three of the four primary classrooms, pupils did much of their work in groups. The organization of groups can be complex. In the following excerpt a primary teacher explains how her pupils were in different groups for different things; this had to be managed in the context of a fairly integrated day:

There's actually four groups [for mathematics]. I could possibly get away with the seven groups in here [a spacious classroom] but . . .

there's so many of them you really just have to do that ... There's
three English groups, well actually four because there's two adjust-
ment groups ... doesn't always follow [that a pupil is in the same
level group for mathematics and for English] the mathematicians
aren't maybe always so good with the English side ... English mainly
to begin with you've just got to base it on the groups you receive
them in [from the previous year]. I keep them rather than changing
everything around to begin with ... Then perhaps I discover they
might be making a lot of progress ... Some children all of a sudden
make leaps and bounds and they can, you know, manage to move
into another group ... I don't think I've ever moved anyone *down* a
group but I've tried to move up a group.

For the project it's a social group. Social grouping is better for
environmental work.

These extracts from the teachers' accounts provide only a taste of the
ways in which teachers' plans and their actual management of their
classroom teaching interacted. We must emphasize again what we said at
the start of this section: the teachers regarded their plans as almost
infinitely flexible and implementation was crucially influenced by the
conditions which impinged on their teaching. Classroom events, behaviour,
performance, availability of resources, could all lead to the teacher readily
changing his or her planned actions or goals in response to the circumstances of the moment. The concept and implementation of a teaching
plan in this context is clearly quite distinctive from the detailed and firm
(even rigid) plans which are necessary for industry where, say, the aim is to
manufacture cars or provide a customer service efficiently. Promoting
pupils' learning through teaching is quite a different kind of productive
process.

Moving from the particular to the general

Extracts of this kind can provide interesting and insightful vignettes of how
individual teachers talk about their classroom teaching. They do not,
however, offer any indication of whether each teacher's account is purely
idiosyncratic, or whether the accounts have common features. Individual
idiosyncratic 'stories' about teachers, of course, are valuable and often fasci-
nating, but our main purpose in this research was to explore the possibility
of coming to some *general* conclusions about the ways in which teachers
talk about, and value, their own teaching. For that purpose, we must
concern ourselves in Chapters 4 and 5 with the features which are common
across the accounts provided by different teachers.

Summary

In this chapter we first explained the strategy which we adopted to help teachers to talk about how they make sense of their teaching. This involved:

- Emphasizing what was good about the teaching, in the eyes of the teachers and their pupils.
- Focusing on specific classroom events which occurred when both teacher and researcher were present.
- Determinedly avoiding the imposition of any researcher preconceptions about good teaching or about how to make sense of teaching.
- Helping teachers to remember what was involved in doing the things they did well, the most important element in this being to interview the teachers very soon after the observed lessons.

We have described how the immediate post-lesson interviews, as the main source of data, were supplemented by one later interview with each teacher about the whole observed unit of teaching and another in which taped extracts and pupil comments were used to seek elaboration on themes emanating from that teacher's own accounts of the teaching. We have also sought in this chapter to give readers some initial sense of the nature and variety of the teachers' accounts of their teaching, focusing for this purpose on three of the themes about which the teachers frequently talked: how they maintain the interest and enthusiasm of their pupils; how they diffuse actual or potential discipline problems; and how their planning interacts with their management of classes and of lessons.

4

Generalizations across teachers: goals and actions

The importance of generalizations

So far we have treated the teachers on whom this research centres as 16 individuals. In this chapter we are concerned to see what is common among those teachers in the ways they think about and evaluate their own teaching. Before we can say anything about those commonalities, however, it is necessary that we discuss some of the more technical issues associated with identifying what is common across teachers. We have endeavoured to make that discussion as straightforward as possible so that readers who prefer not to take our word for it can make judgements for themselves on the likely validity of our findings. The first three sections of this chapter are, however, probably the most 'hard-going' sections of the book. The other four sections are devoted to the substantive findings of the first stage of the research, and these findings provide the start of the framework upon which the rest of our work has been built.

In Chapter 3 we discussed the different aspects of their teaching which teachers talked about. There was considerable variation both in what they identified as having pleased them and in the ways they talked about these things. Data of this kind enabled us to understand something of how each of the 16 teachers, *as an individual*, evaluated and talked about his or her own teaching. But the aim of our research was somewhat broader and we wished to go beyond the individual stories teachers have to tell. Our concern was to use the 16 case studies as a modest start towards the development of an understanding of the professional craft knowledge of teachers *in general*. We aspired, therefore, to a cumulative wisdom about teaching which involves more than just a set of possibly idiosyncratic descriptions of the social world of teaching seen through the eyes of a number of individuals.

What we are saying here is that if such wisdom is to be communicated and ultimately used in other contexts, such as pre-service and in-service teacher education or for curriculum development, then it must be potentially generalizable across teachers. To take an extreme position, if the accounts of teaching imply that each teacher construes his or her own teaching in a unique way, then there would be nothing to be learned by other teachers from those accounts. Something has to generalize to other teachers, or other teaching contexts, if the research is to have any significance for those in different situations and so to make a useful contribution to education. This implies that the analysis of the data must attempt to establish generalizations by seeking common concepts across teachers in the ways in which they evaluate and talk about their teaching.

These generalizations would be expected to relate to such things as the ways in which teachers construe the tasks they undertake and the situations which confront them, how they monitor changes in these situations, and how they process all this information in order to make quick decisions. Establishing such generalizations was particularly difficult since we could not know in advance what kinds of generalization (if any) would be possible, and we had scrupulously to avoid contamination from our own preconceived notions of teaching. Should we, indeed, even use phrases like 'information-processing' and 'decision-making'? How could we minimize the influence on our analysis of well-known models of teachers and teaching which have been developed by 'outsiders' (e.g. process–product, or teacher as classroom manager, curriculum developer, dilemma-resolver, facilitator, critical friend)?

Our use of the term 'generalization' does not imply the probabilistic kind, which arises from the application of statistics to large data sets in, for example, survey research or experimental studies. Approaches of that kind would aim to generalize across the whole population of teachers. The generalizations in this context are better described as naturalistic: they form the basis of hypotheses to be carried on from one case to the next, rather than general laws to be applied across a population. An approach of this sort involves seeking commonalities among the data from different cases (teachers), and then going beyond the simple linkage between cases to an attempt to create a theoretical framework. That framework should make sense (to both the teachers themselves and others) of the teaching encompassed by our research, incorporate our case findings and be amenable to testing in the future with new cases. But theory of this kind will always be in some sense provisional; there is no certainty that future cases will conform to the generalizations generated from past cases. We are not expecting or seeking an elegant, closed, theoretical solution; we are looking for a theoretical framework which will help to make teachers' professional craft knowledge more accessible to everyone, including teachers themselves. The framework is a means of helping to expose and make explicit the tacit knowledge of expert experienced teachers who may well manage and teach their classes in such taken-for-granted and routinized ways that they are unconscious of what they have actually achieved.

Criteria for the analysis

Any attempt to draw out generalizations from data which are as rich and varied as the accounts from these teachers, must aim to conform to certain criteria or standards. If it does not, then there will be no way of judging the validity of the generalizations. There seemed to us to be six criteria which we should try to apply to our analysis.

First, any generalization must be directly supported by evidence. Although this might seem an obvious requirement, it is all too easy and tempting to add key elements which help to create a coherent system of generalizable concepts but are not themselves observable in the data. If they are not, then they must not be included.

Secondly, any generalization has to relate to what is *normal* practice. If it relates only to what a teacher does on rare occasions, then it would not be possible to test whether the generalization is a false one; it could always be argued that nothing can be inferred about its falseness on the basis that it did not feature on any given occasions. Those occasions, it could be claimed, are simply not the 'rare' ones.

Thirdly, where generalizations go beyond one teacher and one occasion, they must be supported by evidence from each teacher and from each of that teacher's lessons. (The term 'lesson' used here includes the period of contact between teacher and pupils, that is the lesson itself and the account provided by the teacher in the post-lesson interview.) The extent to which there are commonalities across teachers, or across lessons by the same teacher is, of course, a matter for empirical investigation.

Fourthly, it may be possible to describe how teachers typically think about their teaching in terms of generalizable but isolated elements. The relationships among these elements, however, must also be identified if the framework is to reflect the rationality of the ways in which teachers perceive situations, make judgements and, in consequence, take action.

Fifthly, the framework of generalizations should not discount any part of the teachers' accounts. It is always tempting, and sometimes legitimate, to select what suits and label the rest as 'diverging from relevant matters'. Because our concern is with a framework which reflects *teachers'* thinking about their teaching, we have no basis upon which to decide that parts of their accounts will be discarded.

And finally, any theoretical account we provide of how teachers think has to be recognized and accepted as a balanced account by the teachers themselves.

These are demanding criteria, and we would not have been surprised if we found ourselves unable to claim that they had been met in full. This would not have disturbed us too much since the major functions of the criteria were to guide our analysis and enable us to detect its weaknesses. Such weaknesses might then be overcome in later stages of the work. In the event, we found we were able to a large extent to meet the criteria. For example, the framework of generalizations we generated accounted for all but a fraction of one per cent of the teachers' statements about their classroom teaching; the framework was applicable across all the teachers and across lessons for individual teachers; relationships among all of the generalizable elements were established; and the 16 teachers involved all claimed to recognize and find helpful the theoretical account of their statements about their own teaching.

Extracting generalizations from raw data

Before describing what it was that seemed to be generalizable across teachers and occasions, however, we should indicate how we moved from concrete data (the interviews with teachers) to a theoretical framework (the generalizations). As far as we know there are no established rules of procedure for this kind of analysis. We endeavoured to be as systematic and self-consciously critical as possible, and generally speaking we conformed to the following pattern:

- We read intensively transcripts of two teachers' statements about the things which pleased them in their teaching.
- We met and tried out together some of our preconceived ideas used in interpreting the transcripts, and then formulated other (half-baked) ideas.
- We read more transcripts to see how the ideas related to the new data.
- We met and bounced ideas off each other.
- We went back to the earlier transcripts to see how our latest ideas 'fitted' the data.
- We rejected or retained ideas and formed them into a set of rough but useful-looking concepts which seemed to reflect some of the ways in which the teachers talked about their teaching.
- We generated questions in terms of these concepts to be asked of each interview or written statement.
- We went back over all the interviews or statements already examined and tried to clarify and sharpen the concepts and questions.
- We recorded data which did not 'fit' the emerging conceptual framework.

- We moved on to the analysis of the rest of the interviews adding further questions and concepts as necessary and recording what did not 'fit' the framework.
- At all stages where amendments or additions were made, we were prepared to 'go round in circles' again to check on our earlier analysis.

Using this inductive, iterative and time-consuming procedure we analysed interviews with all 16 teachers, and interviews on different occasions with the same teacher. Both post-lesson and follow-up interviews were included. From this emerged a set of generalizable and interconnected concepts which encapsulated virtually everything the teachers had to tell us about the teaching we had observed.

These concepts are, of course, second-order concepts; that is, they reflect our ways of representing teachers' perceptions; they are not teachers' own concepts. What was striking, however, was the extent to which they seemed to accommodate what different teachers had to say, what teachers had to say after different lessons, and what teachers had to say after a longer period of time to reflect on the recording of the lesson.

It is perhaps important to note, however, that our inductive approach to the analysis started with the 12 secondary teachers, and their statements were the most influential in establishing our generalizations. The statements from the four primary teachers all fitted in to this structure very well, but we have no way of knowing whether it would have developed in the same way had we started with the primary teachers and had they been a larger sample.

The immediacy of teaching

Regardless of the extent to which one can generalize across teachers, it seems inevitable that the ways in which they construe their classroom teaching must be such as to facilitate rapid decision-making and action. When faced with classes which have lost interest, performed unexpectedly well or become disruptive, teachers have no time to wring their hands, reflect on complex theories of learning or of motivation, and make sophisticated choices between alternative courses of action. They have to act quickly, spontaneously and more or less automatically. Immediacy is the essential characteristic of the situation, and any implicit theory the teacher may use must be such that it can swiftly produce the appropriate course of action.

Our expectation, therefore, was that as a result of their experience the teachers would have established repertoires of routines for themselves. These routines would be called into play as the situation required, and would have been learned over a period of time. Beginning teachers would be unlikely to have such repertoires, and so what experienced teachers take for granted and more or less unconsciously make use of, can be something of a mystery to a student or probationary teacher.

But what is the nature of these 'routines' (if, indeed, they exist)? Do they have features which are common across teachers? Do all teachers use them? Is it possible to unpack their structure and provide concrete examples from the analysis of the statements about their teaching from these 16 teachers? To answer these and our other questions we put the procedure outlined in the previous section into operation.

Normal desirable states of pupil activity

The most obvious common feature of the different teachers' accounts was that in response to our question about *their teaching* they almost always talked about what their *pupils were doing*. Their dominant goals, and the terms in which they first evaluated the lessons, were concerned with establishing and maintaining what we call a *Normal Desirable State of Pupil Activity* (NDS) in the classroom (see Figure 4.1). In other words, the lesson was seen as satisfactory so long as pupils continued to act in those ways which were seen by the teacher as routinely desirable. What was seen as normal and desirable by one teacher, however, could be quite different from the NDS of another. Furthermore, the NDS of one stage of a lesson could change quite markedly as the lesson progressed.

So what was the nature of these normal, desirable states of pupil activity? What kinds of contrasts were apparent among the patterns preferred by different teachers?

The secondary teachers' NDS largely fell into two categories: those characterizing activities where the teacher was interacting with the whole class, and those where pupils were working independently on tasks of various kinds. Genuine 'group work' was rare.

Where pupils were working independently, the pattern of activity which the teacher saw as desirable depended to a large extent on the nature of the pupils' tasks. Even in cases where similar tasks were being undertaken,

---

Normal Desirable State of Pupil Activity (NDS)

- To be established and maintained
- Varies from teacher to teacher
- Varies with stage of the lesson

Figure 4.1 NDS: the dominant generalizable concept used by teachers in evaluating their own teaching

however, different teachers could have different conceptions of NDS. In parallel science classes, for example, each of which was following the same resource-based course and worksheets, two teachers perceived the laboratory activity in different ways.

One of them described her NDS in terms of pupils settling down quickly into the laboratory routine, knowing where and when to seek help from the teacher and technician, and getting on with 'working independently, using the worksheets, doing everything so much on their own'. Her goal was that they would be interested, working hard at their own pace, and making their own discoveries: 'They're all doing it in their own time . . . you can see each one coming to something in the worksheets and discovering something new.'

The second teacher emphasized the continuity and purposeful nature of the activity and the relationship between himself and the pupils:

> The sort of sense of how, the whole thing, there weren't really empty gaps or spaces, you know. It seemed that we started to do something and we kept on doing it right to the end, and there didn't seem to be points where pupils didn't know what to do or felt they were wasting time. A sense of purpose to it . . . they're not here just to play . . . A kind of friendliness, sort of mixed with a sense of humour, kind of relaxed atmosphere. It isn't always there, you know, you have to work at it. That seemed to work from the beginning so that people seemed more, well, it was easier for them to come up with questions or problems . . . they weren't shy about it. If they didn't understand something, they didn't know what to do, then they would come out and do it. I liked that.

Looking across teachers in different subjects, the tasks which pupils undertook in their independent work displayed considerable variation in the extent to which they were structured. This was reflected in the NDSs described and illustrated in the contrasting accounts from teachers of English, geography and mathematics.

The English teacher's NDS was concerned with an open-ended task, associated with work on a novel, and intended to encourage pupils to think for themselves:

> It needed a few more pointers to pinpoint. But the intention of that was to make *them* think about how they would identify with the characters, get them to make up their own minds rather than me imposing this is what you should think about the characters.

In a geography class pupils were given some choice about which task they would undertake. The task itself, however, was highly structured and they were expected to seek the 'right' answer. The teacher was aiming for an NDS in which the pupils used the task as a way of:

Giving them practice in reading and picking out facts from reading, like the one on Sri Lanka, it's got a passage about a tea estate, and they've to fill in the missing words from reading the passage and looking at the pictures.

The mathematics tasks were also highly structured, but in this case there was no choice for the pupils in what they would attempt. During the individual work there was some possibility that as they worked 'on their own' they might work at different rates. However, this teacher's NDS was clearly one in which all pupils were looking back over their previous work (the properties of rectangles) and using it to help with the new work (on squares):

> I can actually line up the properties and they can fill them in themselves for the square . . . [I] gauge how well I put something across by the number of questions that come back to me once they start to work.

Teachers' preferred NDSs also illustrated differences in the social interchange which they aimed to maintain while their pupils were working independently. An art teacher and a history teacher provided an interesting contrast.

The history teacher was clear about the regular pattern of activity for which she was looking. Her aim was for the pupils to be in their places, attending to their tasks rather than their friends and displaying good behaviour and politeness:

> I don't expect talking. I do maintain silence and I think a lot of them just think they can talk when and where they want. Secondly, I don't expect them to be on a Royal walkabout, you know, sort of touring the room the whole time. I don't mind them coming out to the filing cabinet, fair enough, but I think some of them move out of their seats far too easily . . . Basic standards of good behaviour and manners. *I always* expect 'please' and 'thank you' and a hand up . . . I think my views they're not in vogue in teaching at the moment . . . I think there's a trendy sense of being over-familiar to children in some respects. I believe there are standards . . . being polite, being attentive . . . not always constantly chattering . . . working the whole time.

The art teacher was also keen to encourage 'good manners' but her NDS reflected a different approach from the history teacher. This may signal differences either between the two teachers or between subject areas. It may be that art is more appropriately served than is history by the pattern of activity whereby pupils are expected to be relaxed and free to talk to each other, as well as getting on with their work:

It's largely keeping them interested, keeping them going, allowing them a fair bit of freedom . . . without making it seem a chore. Hopefully, they enjoyed the painting. I don't *mind* them chatting a bit. Some of the painting at this stage is obviously fairly automatic so that I don't mind them having their wee conversations as long as they're still working, as long as I can see the brushes still going on the paper, so long as whenever I want to address the class I can do it . . . [I was] less open and chatty today . . . Normally [they] are keen to talk about things like my earrings . . . everyday chat. They'll stop at the desk on the way in and say 'I did such-and-such at the weekend'.

Most of the individual teachers included both whole class and independent working NDSs in their accounts. The French teacher, for example, talking in the context of a language laboratory lesson, described her NDS for this form of independent working. Her aim was for the pupils to be motivated to perform (pronunciation and repetition in the foreign language) accurately, independently and with enthusiasm:

[At] the machines . . . everybody was doing the repetition and doing it properly . . . and they were all taking it seriously to the very end when they were all listening in to somebody else, a joke which they enjoy. In the beginning when they do that exercise they all think it's a laugh, but eventually when they're more used to it they actually listen to how the other people are pronouncing and repeating . . . They like to work things out for themselves, the ones who enjoy it are so keen and enthusiastic and really pleased with themselves when they work something out without being told about it. You can hear them sort of whispering as well 'I said that' . . . It's more satisfying for them . . . If you're keen at something, you're interested in it, you want to know *why* it is. You don't want to just be told. I want them to be sufficiently interested to ask things.'

In describing an NDS for whole class teaching, she reflected once again her aim that pupils should be working things out for themselves, and that all pupils should be in a position to overcome any reluctance to participate and feel themselves a part of the class activity:

I kept getting them to try and get answers for themselves without me giving it straight to them . . . I tried to include everybody . . . [some] don't like to volunteer, because they're frightened, you know, the sort of group pressure if they get it wrong people will laugh at them . . . So I try and ask them things that they're going to be able to answer. If they can't do it, then take that wee bit of extra time and the rest of the class will wait for 30 seconds.

It was not uncommon in the whole class teaching for several different NDSs to be identified in the account of a single lesson. An English teacher, in describing a lesson which focused on the reading of a play, identified two distinctive NDSs. On this occasion the teacher was dissatisfied with the lesson and so we have to some extent to infer the nature of his desired pattern of activity from his account of what did not happen. The first NDS concerned the preliminary work to 'get into the play'. This has two features: first, he implied what he expected of the pupils' behaviour in relation to his classroom management expectations and secondly, he indicated a hope for particular kinds of responses from the class at the start of the lesson to demonstrate their interest in, and understanding of, the play:

> The class came in and settled down quite quickly . . . I *refuse* to start shouting . . . I wait . . . gradually everybody says 'OK, we're about to start work' . . . The teacher must be the central point . . . Going back over the play, recapping, standing procedure, was revealing to me and pointed out that the class had not really put together very logically, or chronologically perhaps, the events . . . Maybe that has been the problem in that they've felt it dragging . . . I was aware that if I wasn't *driving* away at the front, if I stopped talking, it would just break down. They weren't really interested in working.

The second NDS involved the actual reading of the play. The implication of the negative statements was that he was looking for pupils to display enjoyment, interest, amusement and verve in their responses and performance:

> That for me was a nightmare . . . I don't think the children enjoyed it. There I go for the word 'joy' again, but I suppose that's the bottom of it all at the end of the day . . . Halfway through I stopped in the hope of generating some sort of either response from them or interest to get them going again . . . My only solution [was] I took a part myself . . . It worked . . . I think they were more interested . . . Normally a class reacts very well to the play and they pick up the funnies and the little lines. . . . The reading was pathetic . . . It was low, muttery . . . Today they weren't interested at all . . . I would have expected somebody to say 'can we read on?' . . . but nobody did that.

In all cases the several NDSs which the teachers ascribed to each teaching occasion were connected in a rational sequence. In some instances, however, it was the sequence of activities itself which was the particular focus of attention. This was particularly so for the outdoor education teacher in describing an expedition to a river gorge:

> I always try to avoid having long periods without any change, try to do lots of different things . . . to link up a series, like problems of crossing the river on tree trunks, steep hills, small challenges that every

child can do. Part of it is watching the others and the teacher doing it.
I feel I have to do everything the kids do, even the jump into the mud
... Today I fell over into the mud which they enjoyed. I talk about
anything ... ladybirds ... onion grass ... the history of the castle. I
talk to individuals a lot in the bus or when we're walking.

This teacher is keen for the pupils to have a series of memorable experiences and opportunities to see nature from the inside 'like a squirrel in
a tree'. Throughout, however, his aim is to strike a balance between, on the
one hand, feelings of excitement and hints of danger and, on the other
hand, ensuring pupils' safety and confidence in themselves and his support
for them.

Group work was less common than either individual work or whole class
arrangements. This was particularly the case in the secondary school,
although at first sight it did appear to characterize a substantial proportion
of the computing studies teaching. The number of computers available
made inevitable the sharing of each machine among several pupils.
However, the characteristics of the NDS identified by the computing
studies teacher did not suggest any of the specific features, such as cooperation among members or the adoption of particular roles by different
members, which might have been expected in the context of group work.
His description was one of pupils at their machines, involved in the work
and enjoying themselves; it could have applied equally well to individual
work.

For the primary teachers too, group work appeared on the surface to
dominate the teaching. On closer inspection, however, it seemed that each
group could be thought of as operating in two modes: whole class teaching
and independent work. The most common pattern was for the teachers to
organize their class into about three groups and then send two off to get
on with a set of tasks on their own (independent work). The remaining one
stayed with the teacher and was taught as a whole class might be. To maintain this the teacher had to plan and organise the work effectively, and the
pupils had to be prepared to get on with their work by themselves for
longer periods than was required in the secondary school. One primary
teacher described this pattern of activity in the following way:

> The poorest group who were doing the fractions. They got nearly 30
> minutes of me today, which is a fairly hefty whack of the morning, so
> the planning, if you like, in making sure that they would have that
> time, was successful. And the purple group, well it's straightforward
> number work, the decimals, and they were doing dividing numbers by
> hundreds ... That's basically, because they've already done tenths,
> straightforward. I knew more or less I would be leaving them to work
> on their own ... The orange group, the middle group, who were
> doing the shape, the cubes, I thought that was quite successful.

I liked the way they were working on their own and, on the whole solving their own problems. Because built into the page were a few problem-solving techniques and they coped, apart from the initial thing about the size of the card.

It is not, of course, just a question of pupils getting on with their work independently. Teachers are keen that they should have positive feeling about it: 'They quite enjoy doing their maths and they get on with it . . . They get a lot of satisfaction at getting them right.'

In addition, the teacher may delegate some of his or her responsibilities to pupils:

Self-correction is encouraged . . . But there are some children you've got to watch . . . There are children you know will correct it and come out to you and say 'I got that right, I think, I'm ready to move on' . . . You get other children who you really couldn't.

However efficient these teachers are at dovetailing the whole class teaching and independent working of each of the groups, inevitably there will be some pupils who need to ask the teacher for help while he or she is occupied with another group. Some of these demands are dealt with by having gaps between the blocks of the whole class activity, and trying to deal with all the problems of those who have been working independently. Whatever way the teacher manages things, there appear to be 'rules' which develop over time and characterize the pattern of classroom activity; it is expected that pupils will observe these rules in approaching the teacher:

They know not to disturb me if I'm hearing reading . . . They're well into my routine . . . They *know* that at certain times I'm not approachable. And usually if I'm actually teaching in maths, if they see me speaking, they can't approach. But if they see me when I'm marking or checking they know to interrupt. And if I'm on my way to a group they can grab me as well, the rest can wait.

The group activities we observed all involved pupils being grouped according to achievement, although individuals might find themselves in different groups for different kinds of work-number, reading or other language. We were told that for some activities, such as project work, 'social' rather than 'achievement' groups were frequently formed. In all our observations in the primary classrooms, however, we observed none of the cooperative working which was implied by this alternative grouping base. Everything we saw was either whole class or independent working.

We have devoted a substantial amount of the text of this chapter to the illustration of what teachers saw as normal and desirable patterns of classroom activity. The reason for that is that the maintenance of their NDSs was the major goal for the teachers. But, one may ask, what about pupils' learning? Where is the concern for that?

That might be answered in two ways. First, it is important to remember that our concern is with the immediate task of how teachers construe their classroom teaching; although their focus is on activities, we would expect that in their prior planning the intended activity patterns would be determined in part by what they wanted their pupils to learn. Secondly, the teachers' accounts identified a second set of goals, which we have called *Progress*, and pupils' learning was included within this set.

Progress

A second concept, to add to NDS, which was generalizable across the 16 teachers and different occasions was, therefore, that of *Progress*. All the teachers evaluated their lessons not only in terms of maintaining particular NDSs but also in relation to promoting specific kinds of Progress. Progress goals were less numerous than activity goals and, although diverse, fell into three broad categories. First, there was the development of pupils' knowledge, understanding, skills, confidence or other attributes. The second category was concerned with Progress in the sense of generating a product; a performance, artefact or completed exercise. And finally, there was Progress through the work, which might mean accomplishing a sequence of planned activities, getting through a course, or establishing continuity across some kind of transition point.

Before going on to look at these categories we should provide some indication of how the general concepts of NDS and Progress are to be distinguished, and what relationships (if any) there may be between the two.

Our approach to the distinction is based on the assumption that NDS involves something being maintained without change over a period (albeit sometimes a short period) of time; Progress introduces a development aspect which contrasts with the steady state of NDS. In analysing teachers' accounts, unambiguous categorization as NDS or Progress is not always possible. For our purposes this ambiguity is sufficiently rare so as to present no great problem. As an example, however, let us consider a case where a teacher talks about 'pupils understanding'. We would categorize a reference to 'pupils understanding what is going on in the classroom or what the teacher is saying' as NDS. If the concern was with 'pupils developing an understanding of something', however, we would see this as an example of Progress. In some instances we have found teachers talking about 'pupils picking things up' (in the sense of understanding) and we have had some difficulty in deciding how this should be classified.

In any given lesson, it would be expected that there would be some connection between the NDSs and Progress to which the teacher refers. The 'rational curriculum planning model' might suggest that activities

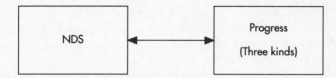

Figure 4.2   The generalizable goals in teachers' evaluation of their own teaching

would be undertaken as a means of achieving a specific kind of progress, and so imply an arrow direction from NDS to Progress (left to right in Figure 4.2). In some instances this was reflected in the ways the teachers talked about their teaching, but that was not always, or even usually, the case. While they were actually teaching, it was often the establishment and maintenance of a particular kind of classroom activity which the teachers saw as the primary goal. Any concern for Progress might be presented either as a quite separate goal or, indeed, as a necessary prerequisite for establishing the activity (right to left in Figure 4.2, going from Progress to NDS). In a resource-based science course, for example, pupils' progress through their worksheet tasks was a necessary facilitator to maintaining their independent systematic pattern of activity in the laboratory. The operation of the whole course was dependent on that activity. In a computing studies course, one of the teacher's major aims was to establish a pattern of classroom activity with the pupils taking instructions equally well from him, from worksheets and from the computer screen. He recognized, however, that they must first make progress in developing their capabilities to take instructions from each of these three sources before he could attain the consistent pattern of activity he was looking for.

Let us now turn to some illustrations of the teachers' Progress goals. One type of Progress goal described by the teachers reflected different kinds of learning or development in pupils. There was emphasis on pupils' cognitive learning, acquisition of concepts, picking up ideas and developing skills. However, there were also numerous examples of pupils' affective growth (confidence and poise) among teachers' priorities, and of concern for such things as pupils becoming capable of thinking through problems for themselves, making their own discoveries and applying their theoretical knowledge to practice:

- 'Well, they've done quite a good period's work and now they at least know about this new number system and can transfer between one and the other . . . Most of them had grasped the concept of the binary system . . . I was only after a transformation between the binary and decimal and the way we go about it.'
- 'I think history is all about learning and finding out and being able to use

books. Whether it's a dictionary, or an encyclopedia, or reference books, and I think again that's a skill.'

- 'The two who sit side by side there, they've become a lot more confident.'
- 'I think that part of the teaching is . . . teaching a child to be aware of their voice and confident enough to speak in class.'
- 'She gets so embarrassed she doesn't want to demonstrate [at PE] . . . Now obviously the ideal would be to get her out of that . . . [in] a fun way round it in as much as the children will start to see her for what she is and then she'll integrate more.'
- 'On a good day it works beautifully. It's like clockwork, and you can see each one of the children coming to something in the worksheets and discovering something new.'

A second, and less frequent, category of Progress relates to the production of something. In some cases it was clear that the lesson, or series of lessons, was devoted entirely to this product. The 'performance' of a play in an English class, and the making of masks in a series of single periods of art, were obvious examples. These, however, were a minority. More common was the goal of getting some kind of task, exercise or worksheet completed:

- 'They get a guided tour there, they have a worksheet to do . . . It's very good, it's very comprehensive.'
- 'I read Graham's out mainly because it had a good description in it and this was what I was trying to get from them . . . I wanted the story, I wanted the narrative, the expressive story, but I also wanted the description . . . Some of them have done very well.'

Making Progress through the work constitutes the third category. A few of the statements which fall into this category indicated progress in the sense of a transition from one lesson to the next, or to some new aspect of work, or across a series of activities over a period of time. For the most part, however, the teachers' goals were concerned with progression through the material or activities which they had planned for the lesson, or through 'the course':

- 'It went fairly well the way it was planned. It was quite a long 'lecture' at the start of the lesson, but I think, you know, I tried to get through what I wanted to in the time . . . you're trying to follow some sort of pattern in their learning and taking them on, progressing each week.'
- 'The boys are actually shooting ahead in their maths. They're going to be finished the primary scheme just after Easter and they will be doing extension work in the summer term.'
- 'Three groups . . . spend one day on reading, or discussion, or both – purely oral work. And the other two days will be spent on an assignment,

or assignments, to do with the story that we've discussed or read together.'

It appeared, therefore, that in the forefront of teachers' criteria for evaluating their own teaching was the maintenance of NDSs and of Progress; the former, however, was given more prominence and described in greater detail in their accounts. We made the point earlier in this chapter that when asked about their teaching teachers invariably responded by talking about their pupils. Notwithstanding this apparent priority, all of them ultimately talked about what they did, and our third generalizable concept we call *Teachers' Actions*.

Teachers' Actions

What was striking about the statements was that despite having been asked a question about 'good teaching', no teacher evaluated any aspect of his or her teaching in terms of it being inherently desirable, as a characteristic of 'good teaching', or indeed in any terms other than as instrumental towards some kind of NDS or Progress. In other words, when they spoke about their own actions the teachers appeared *always* to evaluate them in terms of the extent to which they were effective in maintaining particular NDSs or promoting specific kinds of Progress.

At this stage then we have three interrelated generalizable concepts and we are starting to build a simple theoretical framework which reflects how these teachers construed their teaching. The three concepts of NDS, Progress and Teachers' Actions are shown in Figure 4.3.

The number and diversity of teachers' goals, either NDS or Progress, were relatively manageable when compared with the vast array of different

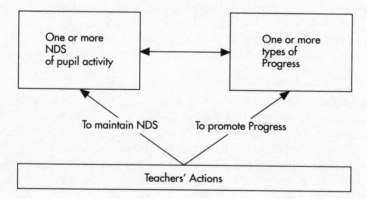

Figure 4.3   Three interrelated and generalizable concepts used by teachers in evaluating their own teaching

actions they described. We can do no more than provide a small number of examples to show something of the relationship between actions and goals, and it is to these examples that the rest of this section is devoted. The first four are concerned with maintaining various NDSs and the last three with promoting Progress.

An English teacher was anxious that pupils should recognize and enjoy the humour in a play (NDS). The Action he took to achieve this was to draw attention to the humour and 'model' an enjoyment response:

> Normally a class reacts very well to the play and they pick up the funnies . . . Now that class really hasn't picked up a lot of the funnies. I've been sniggering at the front. If I laugh the idea is if they see me [they think] 'Why's he laughing?' and they look 'Oh yes, there is something funny there'. They pick it up. I'm not laughing because I think it's terribly funny.

In one of the primary classrooms, the teacher was keen that the pupils would empathize with the people in a story from ancient history (NDS). He wanted them to be interested and to appreciate the links with their own experiences as they sat and listened. The Action he took also included the introduction of humour together with an attempt to get them to draw comparisons between their lives and lives in ancient times:

> I try to bring out the differences in life then and life now and what they would do if they were in the position of the person in the story . . . It makes it that bit more interesting. They cannot focus on something that happened, you know, thousands and thousands of years ago. What they *can* focus on is things that they do and these people do that are *different* . . . I tried to keep the lesson going by including perhaps the odd little bit of humour which I think is important to keep the children interested.

One of the science teachers was aware that for their resource-based arrangement to be effective, the pupils' independent working had to be carried out in an atmosphere of workmanlike calm. If the activity were disruptive things would rapidly get out of hand. He spoke of the importance of a quiet, steady delivery on his part as an appropriate Action to take in one of his lessons:

> [I had] to have a very, very calming influence . . . coupled with my voice . . . It seemed to make things quieter and I think they seemed to respond in a similar way . . . I imagine if I'd been shouting at them it would have kept . . . a more intense atmosphere than it was.

The French teacher was particularly concerned that in the question and answer activity of the class, the lower achieving and less confident pupils would be prepared to volunteer answers. One of the Actions she regularly

took was designed to encourage pupils to attempt to speak in French without fear of ridicule for mistakes:

> I'm trying to get the rest, the ones who haven't had the confidence to
> put their hands up, to try and give their views or opinions . . . A lot of
> them . . . will know only half of it . . . Well, that doesn't matter as far as
> I'm concerned, I'd rather they gave the bit they know . . . [But] you've
> got to build that up, let them know from the beginning . . . The first
> rule, that I always say [to the class], if somebody makes a mistake you
> never ever laugh at them. If you do you're in trouble with *me*.

Turning now to Actions teachers take to promote Progress, one of the
goals of the geography teacher was that her pupils would develop an
awareness that they already had some general knowledge.

> [I] varied the questions a wee bit too . . . I also used this as a chance
> just to make them realize that they do know a little. Because I mean
> that stuff is not stuff I've told them. They rake it out of their own
> minds, the things they know about, the Olympic Games . . . Berlin,
> the Walled City, that sort of thing.

The art teacher was particularly anxious that pupils' Progress in their
imaginative work should not be held back by technical problems associated
with a lack of basic drawing skills. She was prepared to provide a certain
kind of help with their drawing to ensure that they could get on to the
more important things:

> When I was going round the class I was then keeping things going by
> helping them with the technical problems so they don't get stuck . . .
> and then lose interest . . . I think it's better for me to give them some
> help so they don't get stuck, just a few lines of sketch to start . . . If
> you help them a bit with the technical groundwork then they can
> carry on with their own flights of fancy afterwards.

A prominent goal for the outdoor education teacher was that pupils
should develop appropriate behaviour towards the countryside, and understand the extent to which they were behaving in that way. The Action he
took to promote these kinds of Progress included the creative use of pupil
assessment and his own modelling of good behaviour:

> I write a comment about each one at the end of the day and I let
> them see them, you saw them looking. The worst thing I can say
> about someone is that they were a liability that day, and litter is very
> bad. I'm strict about that. I pick up litter we find, I think it's very
> important to show a good model. Some of them often get a very bad
> example from their parents.

The need to extend the framework of concepts

In this chapter we have provided examples to illustrate the general concepts of NDS, Progress and Teachers' Actions, which teachers appear to use in evaluating their own teaching. These three concepts have enabled us to make a start on developing a framework (see Figure 4.3) to describe how teachers think about their classroom teaching. So far, however, we may have given the impression that teachers construe their classroom work in a somewhat clinical way without making reference to the context in which they find themselves. No mention has been made of all the demands, pressures and influences which their environment imposes upon them. But teachers very clearly do include these factors in their thinking about their teaching, and this is reflected in a fourth generalizable concept which we will refer to as the *Conditions* which impinge on the teaching.

Conditions appear to arise from a number of different sources. We have identified five, and find that their influence is manifest in two broad ways. First, they affect the *standards* which teachers can expect in maintaining their NDSs and promoting Progress. Secondly, they may lead to *variation in Teachers' Actions*. The next chapter provides an elaboration of this fourth concept, the relationships between it and the other three and the theoretical framework of generalizations which is formed by these connected concepts. At that stage we find ourselves in a position to say something about the routines which teachers use.

Summary

In this chapter, we have begun to develop a tentative generalized model of how teachers make sense of their everyday teaching. We first explained that our aspiration to formulate theoretical generalizations was necessary as a basis for illuminating teaching other than that which we have studied; and we suggested six key criteria which we had to try to meet in formulating generalizations. We also outlined the collaborative and iterative inductive process through which we generated generalizations. The remainder of the chapter has been devoted to explaining and exemplifying three major concepts for describing how teachers make sense of their own teaching. It is reported that the teachers studied all evaluated their teaching exclusively in terms of their attainment of two general types of goal. The more pervasive of these types is *normal desirable states of pupil activity*, which are steady states of activity seen by teachers as appropriate for pupils at different stages of lessons. The other general type of goal is *Progress*, of which three main subtypes are pupils' learning or development, the creation of products, and the coverage of work. While each teacher appears to depend in monitoring and evaluating lessons on a limited number of these two types of goal, each teacher seems to have a very large repertoire of *Actions* directed towards the attainment of these goals, these actions being evaluated in terms of their success in attaining these goals.

5

The conditions of teaching and a theoretical framework

Factors influencing teaching

The environment in which teaching is carried out has profound effects on what teachers do and the standards they expect to achieve. This is well illustrated and documented in, for example, the experiences of student teachers. It is not unusual for such students, about to embark on teaching practice, to be encouraged to select a set of objectives for a lesson, plan appropriate activities to achieve those objectives and set out to evaluate the extent to which their strategy has been successful. Not infrequently the students return to the college or university after a spell in a school bewailing the fact that teaching is not so straightforward, and their best laid plans have gone awry because of unexpected events, constraints, disruptions and so on. The model they have been given, they often claim, is unrealistic and takes inadequate account of the practicalities of schools and classrooms.

In Chapter 4 we may seem to have been suggesting that teachers' own implicit models of teaching could be represented by a scheme in which they simply select from their repertoire of Actions the appropriate ones to achieve their desired patterns of pupil activity (NDS) or of Progress. If that were the case, then we would be perpetuating an even more unrealistic model than that offered to the students, and misrepresenting the accounts which the teachers gave of their teaching. They were very conscious of the circumstances in which they were working, and of the impact of those circumstances on their teaching.

In addition to the goals of NDS and Progress, and the Teachers' Actions to achieve those goals, we found a fourth concept which was generalizable across teachers and which we refer to as the *Conditions* which impinge

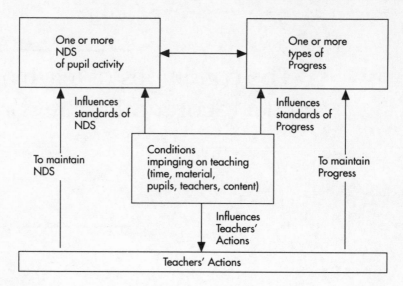

Figure 5.1 The concepts which teachers use in evaluating their own teaching

on the teaching. This concept was to emerge as a crucial element in the teachers' accounts. The Conditions had a profound effect on the *standards* which the teachers felt they could apply in maintaining their preferred NDS or promoting Progress; in some cases standards were lowered, in others enhanced. In addition, Conditions could lead to *variation in the Teacher's Action* taken on any occasion to achieve his or her goals. We had now identified, therefore, four generalizable and interrelated concepts (see Figure 5.1). This completed our framework but there was still a great deal of detail to unpack in its structure and functions, particularly in relation to the Conditions.

With only a tiny minority of exceptions, the teachers' descriptions of the Conditions impinging on their teaching fell into five categories to do with *pupils, time, content, material environment* and *teachers themselves*.

Pupil Conditions

The most salient type of Condition related to the pupils, and Pupil Conditions were of two kinds. The first arose from the behaviours or characteristics which pupils displayed on a particular occasion. For example, a teacher of physical education valued opportunities to involve pupils in demonstrations of basketball skills in front of the rest of the class. At the end of one lesson he reported on why he had felt it necessary to curtail this activity. The obvious discomforture of a pupil led him to revise his expectations of what could be achieved with her in front of the class, and to change his own actions in accordance with this: 'The wee girl was so shy . . . I cut it short, 15 seconds or something, because I realized the minute we started doing it that she was embarrassed.'

In the same lesson, he was trying to get the pupils to make Progress in their thinking about their basketball so that they would arrive at the point where they would be able to link together, in the game, the things they were practising and the issues they were talking about. However, on this particular afternoon he felt this was undermined by the pupils becoming 'switched off' and his expectations of the standards to be achieved were correspondingly depressed:

> The minute we brought in the *think* element, you could see it breaking down for certain children. 'Do I fake or do I pass? Do I get rid of it now?' . . . When it becomes like hard work . . . some of them switched off and just tried to throw the ball.

In another class the computing studies teacher was looking for the pupils to respond enthusiastically, but realized that his sights would have to be lowered because of their apparent fatigue: 'But first year kids they're really, really tired . . . at the end of the period they were so tired that you can't really sort of tap their knowledge, as it were.'

Disruptive behaviour by individuals or groups is not an uncommon condition to impinge on teaching. A science teacher, for example, explained how he changed his regular pattern of action in response to giggling which had broken out:

> We had giggling girls over in the corner. I find . . . if you go for a kind of block attack on them and say 'Everyone's got to stop giggling' it gets worse and worse. But to make small statements, sort of reduce the tension, it seems to me it's often a tension thing, to make little jokes or whatever then it sort of brings it down. And then after that to say 'I would like *you* to do *this*'. I did that with one girl, I said 'Today you've *got* to do this check-test' and she did, and that calmed things down.

Other teachers referred to pupils being fidgety, bored, hesitant, unmotivated, absent, excited, subdued, 'high', embarrassed, disruptive (as they arrive from another class), over-enthusiastic, bewildered, noisy, chattering, fussing, affected by other events outwith the classroom and losing interest. For the most part, these behaviours tended to reduce the standards of NDS or Progress which the teacher expected to maintain, or to cause the teacher to change tack and try to establish a new NDS or Progress goal. Occasionally teachers mentioned that pupils performed better, grasped ideas, worked more quickly or generally managed their tasks more effectively than had been anticipated. In these circumstances, the standards expected of the NDS or Progress were raised.

In all the examples of pupil Conditions identified so far, the teachers have been *reacting* to some kind of 'sign', from individuals or the class as a whole, about their feelings, state of mind, physical well-being or cognition *on the day*. Although the teachers made frequent mention in this way of how pupils' immediate classroom behaviour imposed Conditions on their teaching, they referred more often to pupils' more enduring characteristics. An English teacher, for example, in describing how he would have preferred that pupils had a more relaxed and free transition from an oral to a written mode of NDS, commented on the characteristics of some of his pupils. These characteristics were well known to him and caused him to ensure a rather controlled pattern of classroom activity. His approach was *proactive* in the sense that he was alert to, and took steps to minimize, possible problems (that is not to say, of course, he would not be prepared to *react* to behaviour inconsistent with his conception of the pupils' qualities):

> At the back of my mind is always this point if somebody like Ian and these three here break out . . . they create mayhem if they really get underway . . . [so I] you know, keep the lid on.

The history teacher also referred to a pupil with known disruptive tendencies, and her preparedness to take action in relation to him in ways rather different from those she took with the rest of the class:

> I don't expect to have to check them about talking out of turn, or being noisy, or moving out of their seats. Reflecting on it, I honestly do not think that many, apart from John . . . are malicious children. But John is going to be, or is *already*, a behavioural problem . . . Came with a terrible [record], I mean I know a lot about him because I'm their Guidance teacher.

The French teacher was anxious to maintain an NDS in which pupils were enjoying the work, picking up the points of the lesson and volunteering answers to her questions. But she viewed some pupils as brighter than others, or as always working faster, and this influenced the standards she expected. It also influenced her own Actions in areas such as the amount of time she was prepared to spend with different individuals:

> Some of them are quite bright, the two girls at the front there. They'll pick anything up . . . There's a wide spread in the class though, which makes it difficult. For example, the boy over there, you need to take a lot of time with him . . . it takes him ages . . . [and] the rest are getting fed up . . . The ones that are a bit poor don't like to volunteer because they're frightened that, you know, sort of group pressure, if they get it wrong people will laugh at them.

Sometimes, as illustrated by one of the science teachers' accounts, adjustments of standards for different pupils were concerned not only with *levels* of Progress, but also with *what* is learned. This is reflected in the Teachers' Actions through the provision of differential help. The teacher discriminates not just in how much help is given, but also in what the help is on:

Rather than them [the more able pupils] being helped [by her] to read the worksheets through, you're spending more time with them showing them how to set up the equipment, how to do certain things, or if you see something else on the microscope you're bringing that out, and you're showing them. Now you wouldn't do that with the other ones. You'd want to stick to the absolute basics with them, what's on the worksheets.

In cases where the teacher sees it as important that all pupils make the *same* Progress, there are prices to be paid. A teacher of English commented on the production of a piece of creative writing and suggested that the variation among pupils in their ability to work fast ensured that only some would have the chance of another enjoyable activity (reading with pleasure):

One of the problems always is when you've got . . . the quick and the slow workers. It's always a bit dodgey as to whether you carry on something the next day, which means that you're going to have quite a few with a gap with nothing really significant to do. So they sit and they read and they always get the pleasure . . . Whereas the poor old slow learners are always catching up with them.

Among the enduring individual pupil characteristics which teachers perceived as important, and as influencing the standards of the NDS and Progress, were ability (general and specific), attention-seeking, self-confidence, lack of interest, motivation, tenacity, attentiveness, gender, maturity, attitudes, disruptive tendencies, shyness, laziness, poor grasp of English, noisiness and reticence. Some teachers clearly place most emphasis on what they see as permanent characteristics of their pupils, while others' accounts of their teaching attend much to pupils' behaviour on the day.

Time Conditions

A second Condition which the teachers identified as impinging on their teaching was *time*. This Condition influenced the NDSs, Progress and Teachers' Actions in a number of ways. In the first place, the time-of-day and, to a lesser extent, the time-of-the-week at which the lesson occurred were crucial. The standard of pupil activity (NDS) or the Progress which could be established and maintained first thing on a Monday morning, could not be accomplished at the end of a Thursday afternoon. As one science teacher put it:

> Today they didn't need to be calmed down . . . because they come in at the *beginning* of the day . . . They come in at the *end* on Wednesday and I find with a lot of classes this does make a big difference. The last two periods they're tired, they've done a lot of things, they want to go home, whereas in the morning they do have different attitudes. Of course, some of them are a little sleepy, they haven't actually woken up . . . [but] they're *waking* up, that's the difference.

It is not only extremes of timetabling in the day, however, which have impact on teaching. Several teachers described how having a class immediately after the mid-morning break (at which, it seems, a variety of exciting and disrupting things can occur), or following some other lesson with a particular colleague, could affect their chances of being able to maintain their preferred NDS or to promote Progress.

A second way in which the timetabling can influence the NDS arises from the time allocation to each lesson. So, for example, an art teacher whose contact with the class was never for more than 40 minutes found her goal of involvement of all pupils, including the weakest, constrained by her need to press on in a short lesson:

> If I have longer with that kind of lesson to do it, then I can get the very weakest ones involved hopefully much more . . . You can wait for a few more hands to go up . . . rather than taking the first answer just so that you can keep the momentum going . . . It's always a balance and every time every set of factors alters that balance, and if you've got a double period and lots of space and lots of time then you can relax, take more time, alter the balance. If you haven't you have to push on.

Even with more adequate timetabled time, however, teachers find that on occasions they are conscious of rushing the activities through. As teachers of French and Geography commented:

> I kept getting them to try and give answers themselves without me giving it straight to them . . . I felt "Oh God, hurry up and get on, get the proper answer" . . . We got bogged down . . . because I was rushing to finish off the lesson.

> I think probably if I hadn't been in a hurry to rush through this, I might have let them have the map in front of them for a while, to let some of the slower ones get it.

On the other hand, teachers were also conscious of how time could facilitate the activity pattern. One primary teacher remarked:

I think the best thing about this morning was that . . . [we] had time. I knew it was going to be one of those days where I would need time for that group and I got nearly 30 minutes with them which is unusual . . . The reading groups, I don't normally do them all in the morning . . . but I managed to get through all of them.

She went on to say how the availability of a continuous period of time with her pupils enabled her to make Progress through the work:

A Tuesday morning is a good morning to come. We have a busy morning but there's no [interruptions]. Tomorrow we have television which is more sort of an interruption, and some go to [the remedial teacher] too. But Tuesday is a good day. We can get through a lot on a Tuesday. I find I've got to plan a Tuesday quite well ahead to fit in everything.

Two other aspects of the Condition of time were illustrated by an English teacher: first he identified the possibility that teachers may find themselves faced with too much time, and secondly he pointed to the problems they can face when something goes wrong with the class activity and there are only seconds available in which to decide what to do. He had found himself in a position where the pupils' interest, attention and involvement, which characterised his NDS, were flagging:

Obviously, while you're teaching one has to think very quickly about what you're going to do about that, and you can't think [too much about] *why* this has happened . . . The immediate problem is: What do you do to get out of the hole which you've got yourself into? . . . With at that particular time something like another 40 minutes to go . . . Although I knew what I was going to do was to finish up with some written work, I still had to get to that point. One cannot suddenly say 'Right, we'll stop reading, get your books out we'll do some written work' because that compounds the felony, as it were, and makes it worse . . . [Later on] the transition to the written work was successful but hurried . . . on purpose to keep everybody occupied because at that point there was still . . . 25 minutes anyway to go. Still a long, long time with a frisky, unsettled class.

Several of these examples demonstrate that Conditions of time lead to variation in Teachers' Actions. They are conscious of constraints which cause them to rush things, or of being tired at the end of the day so that they do not behave with the enthusiasm they like to bring to their classrooms.

In particular, short lessons of 40 minutes can result in a teacher moving out of his or her normal pattern of action. The art teacher explained why she provided help for a pupil whom she would usually expect and encourage to resolve her own difficulties without assistance:

> Today . . . there was one pupil who asked for help and I was quite surprised because I reckon she *can* do it. But I think she was feeling a little bit nervous about it and pressurized. She knew what she wanted to do but she couldn't quite manage it in the time.

Another 40 minute lesson found an English teacher aware that she had distorted the combination of actions she would like to have taken. She felt she had not been able to give the pupils an adequate opportunity to reflect on and appreciate the two pieces of work she had read out to them:

> I felt there wasn't going to be enough time either for me to have looked over them carefully enough to really think what I wanted to stress about them. And I was rushing, I wasn't allowing perhaps enough time for them to sit and think.

Content Conditions

Different kinds of *content* of the teaching were also seen as Conditions which influenced the nature and standards of NDS or Progress. So, for example, the outdoor education teacher was keen to sustain a variety of activities for the pupils, and to take the opportunity to engage individual pupils in extended conversation. On an expedition to a river gorge he found himself able to achieve the first of these very well. On a hill walk, however, he was not, although it provided a much more conducive context for maintaining the individual conversations.

A French teacher described how the particular content of a lesson meant that the pattern of pupil activity had to be responsive and attentive, rather than independent and creative:

> It was all new stuff so . . . I was doing most of the talking, most of the explaining and they were . . . doing the reading and the repetition and answering some questions. But once we're into the lesson more, and they've gone over the new stuff, then the onus is on them far more.

In a primary classroom the teacher felt that her standards, which did not allow for pupils charging round the classroom, were undermined by the need to cover content which had been left incomplete by a student teacher: 'We've had an awful lot of . . . loose ends that had to be tied up . . . so that would account for the awful lot of movement.'

Progress also can be constrained by the content. The computing studies teacher was aware that the content of the worksheets he was using put limitations on the Progress which individual pupils were able to make. In a lesson devoted to developing an understanding of the binary system he commented:

> I went to a couple of people who were at the stage of wondering about more information. The chap who wondered what would happen if you went to 32 . . . The worksheet doesn't cover what happens if you go above the number that you've got.

Content is not, of course, always a constraining factor. The art teacher was aware that by nesting a drawing within a varied set of tasks directed towards the production of a mask, she had used content in a way which encouraged the pupils to make Progress:

> They were quite keen to get back to their drawing. When they came in there were no grumbles about 'Oh, this thing again'. Whereas if it had been a straight drawing without any added interest, they might not have been so keen to get back to it.

And a history teacher, who looked for an NDS in which pupils were interested, lively and enthusiastic in their whole class activity, suggested that the content of her material would influence what she could expect of them:

> Because the nature of the course is such that you have to introduce very briefly the idea of primary and secondary sources and the idea of time. The idea is just to give them a taster and then move on to the Roman stuff. Probably because it's the start of a new topic, it is a wee bit dry . . . As it goes on, you know, things about the Roman baths or the amphitheatre is *much* more interesting . . . When we got to the Roman soldier they were much more interested.

The content of a particular lesson may be distinctively different from the general run of that teacher's lessons and so influence his or her actions. This was illustrated by the teacher of mathematics as she explained how her classroom behaviour changed when dealing with a lesson on the properties of rectangles:

> Usually I put a variety of questions that they're going to meet later on. [But] not this time, I've just given them a list of properties and sort of roughly . . . shown them how they actually work by turning the shapes round. But again this is a *specific* unit, it's a lot of class teaching with this one, most of our units are nothing like that. Most of it is maybe a short 5 minute lesson, 10 minutes going over something that they might meet, that might give problems, and then they come and get the stuff corrected.

Rather more opportunistically, a primary teacher observed how the content of some of his work with an older group within his class released him to do other things:

> The activities today involved a lot of folding and cutting, and there-fore I didn't really need to supervise that as it was older children . . . I started off the lesson by deliberately folding something wrongly . . . [so they would see] it must be folded exactly, and cut exactly, and after that I didn't have to check on that again. So it really was a bonus, it wasn't built into the lesson, it was just something that I noticed as I was going along. I'm not needed here when that's happening, and I had a quick nip round . . . and I could just check [the other groups].

Material Conditions

Not surprisingly, the teachers also saw the *material resources* which they have (or have not) as imposing Conditions on their teaching. It was interesting, however, that these Conditions appeared to play a lesser role in their accounts of classroom events than they do in more general rhetoric about the job of the teacher. A reason for this, however, may be that by the time the teacher reaches the classroom, he or she has already become resigned to making the best of what is available, and we would not infer from our findings that improvements in such resources do not have a high priority among teachers.

One aspect of material resources mentioned was the size of class. A mathematics teacher explained how the disruptive influence of a newly arrived pupil on the class activity was exacerbated by an inconvenient increase in numbers and a need to squeeze an extra desk into the classroom:

> Because she's late entry to the class, she takes the number over the number of desks I really have in my room . . . [It] accommodates 30 and she makes it 31. So I had to get an extra desk put in for her at the side. Now because she was new I let her, if people were off, actually move into the body of the class, because she sticks out like a sore thumb sitting on her own.

On the other hand, the outdoor education teacher showed an appreci-ation of having responsibility for a smaller group on an expedition into the countryside when the pattern of activity could involve pupils being not only excited but occasionally fearful:

> I have to decide who really needs help . . . It is much more difficult when you get above 10. We had 13 today. But even with 13 you have much more time to notice individuals than teachers with a class of 30.

The French teacher appreciated the contribution made by the language laboratory equipment to the maintenance of her NDS. However, the fact that only half the class could use the laboratory at any one time was a constraining factor on the Progress made (it would have been much more constraining had she not had the services of a young French Assistant to take the other half of the class):

> I felt simply because the machines were working all right, apart from just at the end, everybody was doing the repetition and doing it properly . . . I was able to sort of listen in on each one, and they were all taking it seriously to the very end when they were all listening to somebody else, a joke which they enjoy . . . It's a bit easier when they get on to the workbook because there's a lot of exercises that you can go over and use the material. But in the beginning you can't do that because we need to start the exercises with the whole class at once rather than half of them doing it and then the rest coming in and saying 'Oh we've done that'.

Like the language laboratory, the size of the school bus caused problems. The history teacher commented:

> They certainly have a visit to Hadrian's Wall which they've all done [in class]. The only problem is only half of each class has been out because we can only take half in the minibus.

The computing studies teacher might have benefited from an individualised arrangement like a language laboratory. He described the difficulties in maintaining his NDS when pupils were working in groups on a task in which the computers produced sounds:

> You always have a problem when there's so many work-stations working at once. They're all trying to produce sound and I think people get a wee bit turned off . . . Maybe they didn't concentrate too much on their own machine when there was so much going on. If one machine starts a particular tune, and they haven't reached that part, then you know the way the room's set out then they're going to direct their attention over to somebody else's work.

So far, the material Conditions described could probably be improved by an injection of extra funding. Some cases, however, would not require that; they reflect circumstances over which the teacher does have some control. The same computing studies teacher, for example, referred to the layout of his classroom which has to accommodate group work on the computers, traditional whole class teaching and individual 'pencil and paper' tasks:

> I'm wondering whether the desk area should be closer to the blackboard . . . I'm not used to dealing with teacher talk where you can't

really impose yourself on the pupils. It's OK, it's really easy, when they're sitting in a full class, separate seats . . . but when they're in a different shape . . . not all having me in their line of vision. Now I think it *can* work like that but maybe I should be closer . . . especially [to] people who are facing to the side up at the back. It's too easy for them not to look at me.

There are other examples of material Conditions which are unlikely to be influenced either by extra funding or action taken by the teacher. For example, the outdoor education teacher's NDSs are crucially affected by the weather:

I leave the real mud activity till the last and then we go down to the bottom of the gorge to wash off the waterproofs. If it is raining, I have to leave it out because they have to wear their waterproofs to walk back to the bus.

He also had to vary his own actions in response to changes in the environment which were outwith his control:

I didn't spend so much time talking about the history of the castle . . . It was particularly good when we could get inside but now it's boarded up . . . So I decided the best thing to do was move on.

One of the English teachers provided a second illustration of how the environment in which teachers find themselves can influence their actions. He was on the point of staging a gang fight as part of a play but changed his mind:

I thought 'Well, shall I try it in the limited room here?' which would have meant pushing desks back and all the rest of it . . . [but] the carry over of such a thing is basically not worth it. Now what I might well do in another situation like that is go down the Hall, on to the stage, where there's room and space and . . . you wouldn't be a claustrophobic cauldron. That's if you can get in before the other departments.

Teacher Conditions

The last group of Conditions alluded to in the accounts of the teaching referred to the *teachers* themselves. Their emotions, unintended behaviours, habits and other characteristics were seen as having enhancing (rarely) and detrimental (more frequently) effects on the standards of the NDSs and Progress.

One major concern here was with the 'unintended' teacher's behaviour on the day. Such behaviours were perceived, for example, as unnecessarily prolonging a particular activity, rushing things through or failing to provide adequate guidance:

- 'I was spending a long, long time going over points . . . the pace was too slow.'
- 'A fault I have, I tend to become over-enthusiastic and get carried away, as indeed I did this morning. I forgot [the time].'
- 'It's something I've noticed in myself, that somebody starts to give an answer . . . and sometimes I cut them off before they're actually finished . . . which is not good because they should be allowed to finish off what they're saying.'
- 'I was leaving it too vague for them.'
- 'The game was far too short at the end. I had run over my time. I had mis-timed it altogether.'

Quite often teachers mentioned how tired and exhausted they were and how this could affect things. Frequently such comments were linked to the time Conditions since they referred to teaching carried out in the later part of the day:

- 'And so *much* of the time you feel like this at the end, absolutely wrung out, exhausted, *especially* in the afternoons.'
- 'They are normally "high", and what I've got to watch when I'm doing it, because I tend to be a bit "high" myself last thing in the day, is that they don't go over the top.'
- 'Today I didn't have the energy to do that . . . to tackle the class and start saying "come on". I just didn't feel that was on today.'

Others mentioned more enduring features of themselves or their job which could be influential:

- 'Part of it is because I'm so small. I had big arguments with one of the teachers last year who set up the system. *He* likes to move around, but I said "Well it's all right for you, you're six feet" . . . [But] I'm lost as soon as I move away from that chair and the kids have to know where to find you.'
- 'So what's my biggest problem sometimes? *We* [teacher and Head of Department] wrote it out by hand. *They* can't read our writing. Half the questions I'll get say "What does that word say?" . . . It puts you in your place.'
- 'Just one of those hectic days when I'm dragged away to the phone . . . I spend the next couple of days coping with the mistakes that the children think they've solved on their own and haven't.' (Headteacher in a small primary school)

One interesting example of a teacher Condition, and we shall return to this in Chapter 6, reflected the fact that teachers have multiple, and sometimes incompatible, goals. For example, a teacher of English was, on the one hand, trying to be just and fair in allocating pupils parts in a play. On the other hand, his NDS at this stage was one in which the play should be moving along with pupils interested, involved, responsive and attentive. In trying to achieve his first goal he ended up with actors who read poorly and profoundly reduced the standard of his NDS:

> I was maybe trying to be too *fair* by parcelling everything out. Trying to prove how *just* a man I am . . . I thought the more people that do it, if I don't interfere then it will go. But it didn't.

It was clear that the teachers' states of mind affected their own actions. The computing studies teacher contrasted his behaviour in contexts where he felt he was, and was not, in control of things:

> [If] you were totally on top of the situation then you might, you know, try and bring in a wee bit of humour to make things a wee bit more friendly. But if you're not on top of the situation, then that's a very dangerous thing to do, you know, because it starts the ball rolling, as far as the silly-billies are concerned.

A science teacher was aware that having provided the same explanation on several occasions during a resource-based unit, he felt more practised, secure and competent. In consequence, he was able to generate a different and better form of explanation in subsequent interactions with pupils:

> The advantage was having explained it to the others perhaps 10, 12 times, by the time I got to him I knew exactly what to say and how the other people were coping with it. Because this is all new material that we're doing, we haven't done it before. So he was getting a refined, distilled explanation which, I think, made it clearer.

At a very human level, one of the primary teachers told us something of the influence of her personal feelings on her actions:

> It's only when I get a bit annoyed that I tell somebody to move. They know when I'm annoyed and say 'Will I take my desk?' . . . and if I say 'Yes' they know I'm not kidding, that I'm fed up.

The state of play

At this stage, then, we had added the generalizable concept of Conditions which impinge on the teaching to the other generalizable concepts in our theoretical framework. We had organised the Conditions into the categories of pupils, time, content, material conditions and teachers, but we were aware of overlap among these categories and of individual teachers' propensities to include some, but not others, in their accounts of their teaching. We found ourselves at the point of making two major steps forward.

First, we had tentatively produced a theoretical framework of interrelated concepts which was grounded in teachers' accounts of their own teaching. This framework is represented in Figure 5.1 (see p. 70) and reflects our findings that all 16 teachers with whom we worked evaluated their teaching in terms first, of maintaining some kind of *Normal Desirable State of pupil activity* in the classroom, and secondly, of promoting specific sorts of *Progress*. All of the *Teachers' Actions* were directed towards maintaining these activities (NDS) and Progress, although the particular activities and progress varied from teacher to teacher. A necessary additional concept, however, was that of the *Conditions* impinging on the teaching. More specifically pupil characteristics, time, content, material conditions or the teacher's own feelings and behaviour could all constitute Conditions which could affect both the standards which teachers could expect in pupils' NDSs or Progress and the patterns of the Teachers' Actions.

Our second step forward, following directly from the first, was to say something about the nature of the routines which teachers bring into play spontaneously in their everyday classroom teaching. The theoretical framework suggested the following definition for the routines which teachers develop through their experience in classrooms:

A Routine is a standardized pattern of action which a teacher undertakes, recognizing that certain conditions are impinging on his or her teaching, in order to maintain particular desired states of pupil activity or to promote specific kinds of progress.

To put it less formally, we are suggesting that experienced and expert teachers:

- Arrive at the class with clear goals for the pattern of activity (NDS) and for the Progress to be made by the pupils.
- Make rapid initial judgements about the Conditions impinging on the teaching, based on (a) cues which are evident on the occasion, and (b) knowledge they already have about pupils, the environment, the curriculum and themselves.
- Quickly select from their repertoire of Actions those which their experience tells them are best suited to achieve their goals in the given Conditions.

or alternatively modify or replace their goals.

This sequence is largely automatic and repeated many times throughout the lesson as different routines (characterised by goals, Conditions and Actions) are brought into play in the light of the judgements the teacher makes about the circumstances facing him or her. It reflects the immediacy of teaching, and implies that 'planning' for teaching has to be of a particularly flexible nature.

It was not enough, however, for us as researchers to identify a set of second order concepts of this kind which, to our satisfaction, provided an adequate account of the ways in which the teachers talked about their teaching. If the concern was with the *teachers*' perspective on things, then it was necessary that the framework of concepts had meaning for, and was acceptable to, the teachers themselves. In other words, a validation of the framework had to be carried out with those who provided the data for that framework.

Teachers' reactions to the findings

One of the problems of this exercise concerned the form in which the material should be fed back to the teachers. On the one hand, if it was presented as a highly abstract theoretical structure, it might well have been rejected no matter how appropriate its substance. On the other hand, there was little point in offering the teachers data from their interviews without any significant restructuring. Acceptance of that could not be taken as implying acceptance of our theoretical framework.

The approach we decided to use in our validation process started with the construction of 'stories' about each teacher's lessons. These stories were based on the post-lesson interviews but structured as a series of short 'chapters'. Each of these chapters reflected one or more of the concepts of the framework shown in Figure 5.1 and the relationship between them, i.e.:

- Pupils' classroom activity.
- Conditions influencing the standards of pupils' classroom activity.
- Progress.
- Conditions influencing the standards of progress.
- Relationship between the pupils' classroom activity and progress.
- Teacher's Actions to maintain pupils' classroom activity and progress.
- Conditions leading to variation in the Teacher's Actions.

These 'stories' were given back to the teachers, and we explained what had led us to reorganize and interpret what they had said in the interviews and so to produce the 'stories'. The teachers were then asked to comment as fully as possible on the 'stories'. Did they find them intelligible? Did they recognise them as their own thinking about their teaching? Had the researchers distorted what had been said to them? Did the 'stories' give an adequate account of what had been said, and had they missed anything out?

The procedure used for this part of the study involved two interviews with each teacher. On the first occasion, we gave the stories to the teachers, pointed out to them that we had restructured the accounts they had given us in the earlier interviews, explained how we came to use particular concepts in our reorganization of the material, described what we meant by these concepts and provided them with transcripts of their original interviews. We identified the questions (above) which we wished to ask them about their reactions to the 'stories' about their teaching and, after answering any questions they had, arranged a longer interview to take place about one week later. Each teacher was given a written sheet which covered the same ground as the verbal guidance in this first interview.

On the second occasion, the teachers were again asked the questions about whether or not they found our interpretation of what they had said intelligible, acceptable, recognizable, adequate and without distortion. Their responses were fluent and full. Only a small amount of repetition of the questions and probing of the answers was required.

The responses of the 16 teachers to their 'stories' were remarkably favourable. It might be argued that they were 'just being polite', but statements like the following gave us cause for optimism:

- 'I recognized it as being the way I was trying to work.'
- 'The main bones of what really mattered came through.'
- 'This puts it down in a formula I can recognize.'
- 'It's a very fair framework about how I think and go about teaching the lesson.'
- 'A very fair summary of what I intended.'
- 'It's typical of what I do, an acceptable interpretation.'
- 'I recognized it immediately, no difficulty at all.'
- ' "Yes" in a word.'
- 'An accurate account, a true reflection.'
- 'I like the way you compartmentalized it, it made it clearer than just my gabble.'
- 'Quite happy with what was written.'
- 'What you've written about the relationship between the activities and the progress – it's absolutely right. That's the way I see it.'
- 'I recognized it very easily. I think you made it more coherent, gave it a logical pattern.'
- 'It was to my liking – concise and accurate.'
- 'It didn't distort, nothing seemed out of place, nothing was twisted.'

It seemed that no-one was unhappy about our restructuring of what they had said; fitting their statements into the common framework of concepts did not seem to them to have had a distorting effect and several claimed that we had given them a clearer picture of what they had been trying to tell us about their teaching on that occasion. In no case did a teacher see our account as inadequate or as having 'missed the point' of what they were trying to say.

In particular, the concept of the Conditions which impinge on teaching was received with enthusiasm. The 'stories' did not include the subcategories of this concept (pupils, time, material environment, content and teacher) since their inclusion would have broken up the narrative. During the interview, however, these categories were identified and the teachers were asked whether they were appropriate and sufficient. Everyone regarded all the subcategories as recognizable, important and 'ringing true'; most provided examples of how such conditions affected what they did in their own classrooms.

Although individuals may not have mentioned all the different kinds of condition in their interviews, each was adamant that all would be applicable to their teaching at some time. There was, however, one teacher who expressed doubts about the 'teacher' subcategory. Although she accepted that 'a severe emotional upset or tiredness' might make it difficult for a teacher to cope, she indicated that she felt 'strongly that how the teacher feels should *not* affect how you teach. Even on an "off-day" you're paid to do the job, even if you're feeling grotty.'

At this stage it seems reasonable to be optimistic about the validity of our framework of concepts. We had established to *our* satisfaction that it was applicable across the 16 teachers as they evaluated their own teaching. The evidence further suggested *the teachers* found the framework acceptable and, in some cases, helpful. However, some individuals maintained that they might have said quite different things about their teaching of different classes or the same class at a different time. Others used the opportunity to provide more information about the way they thought about their teaching. Sometimes this arose because the teacher wanted to balance something which he or she felt had had too much emphasis in the earlier interviews. We examined these new statements to see if they would indicate a need to modify or extend our framework.

It appeared that the 'new' information could all be contained within the existing framework. The function of this added detail seemed to be to elaborate the picture we already had of the teachers' thinking about the observed lessons, or to extend the teachers' account to their teaching in other contexts. One teacher, for example, felt she had not adequately made clear the importance she attached to being realistic in her expectation of standards. She wanted the pupils to achieve to the 'best of their ability' but could not expect the same high standards from everyone. Furthermore, she wanted to add to what she had already said the point that her expectations of her pupils, and the ways in which she behaved herself, were constrained by the quality of the tools she had to work with. These elaborations fell clearly within our concept of the Conditions ('pupil' and 'material' subcategories) which can influence the standards that can be achieved in maintaining the activities or promoting the progress.

She went on to describe how her aims for classes of older pupils would concentrate on developing their independence from her and the ability to think for themselves. This contrasted with her intentions for the pupils in the younger group whom she encouraged to ask for help so that they would acquire a basic repertoire of technical skills and avoid getting stuck or left behind. Her account illustrated nicely the ways in which the change of goals for the older pupils introduced changes in the kinds of NDS and Progress, and involved corresponding changes in her own actions in order to sustain a new and different Normal Desirable State of activity in her own classroom. All of these new elements, however, fitted comfortably into our framework.

The general agreement we found about the crucial importance of the 'Conditions' impinging on the teaching was reinforced by a range of new examples. There was no difficulty in placing these within our existing sub-categories and they helped to flesh out the distinctions we were making. It seemed that their new awareness of our categorization helped the teachers to articulate more fully their own conceptions of their teaching.

Although the questions asked of the teachers were designed simply to get them to comment on the validity of the framework, a few took the discussion further. In some cases, they commented that the structure of the 'stories' had identified for them specific characteristics of their thinking about their teaching of which they had not previously been conscious. Individual teachers mentioned an undue emphasis on content, the importance of continuing classroom activity, an unacknowledged fear of a particular class, the use of understatement (when she said 'reasonably quiet' she meant 'absolutely quiet, totally attentive') and a great dependence on routine. Almost all the teachers seemed to have been stimulated by their 'stories', to think more deeply about their teaching. One expressed this in a very explicit and positive way:

> I found it fascinating taking time to assess things. It's good experience to sit and think through. I was against the project at first because if pupils pick you out it probably means it's for all the wrong reasons. But it's been a valuable experience to think things through. It's given *me* a framework. I feel a lot of teaching is intuition, practice. Perhaps it's a good time after 10 years to stop and think '*Why* do I do that? Do I always do that?' I've always been wary of passing things on to students [student teachers], but having had a chance to think about it now I'm less nervous about making suggestions.

This teacher introduced a tenuous link between our framework and her communications with student-teachers. Another teacher drew particular attention to the problems students have because they lack background information about pupils. He commented:

> I know, in some cases, even the [pupils'] families. I don't know how we're going to get over to students the importance of building up

background information. Without it they'd be at a loss. When you're in college you're taught to teach from A to Z and then walk out. On that day that certainly didn't happen.

A majority of the teachers identified inadequacies in what they perceived as the current practices for the preparation of teachers. Comment was made that:

- The 'scientific approach' to teaching gave the student a good grounding in lesson preparation but not on *how* to present the material.
- The emphasis was on sticking to a lesson plan but the reality demanded that the teacher be prepared to *change* direction or pace or subject matter as necessary and frequently.
- Students were not prepared for the inevitable interruptions that disrupt the pattern of intended progress.
- They would get a shock when they faced the 'seamier side' of things.
- A formal 'aims and objectives' approach may have a place in planning the work of a class but it is divorced from the reality of how teachers think about their actual teaching.

In response to a direct question about whether our framework of concepts would be helpful to a beginning teacher, most of the teachers gave a cautious 'yes'. It was suggested to them that a student might be able to use the framework while observing experienced teachers at work. It might encourage a better understanding of how the teacher acted to maintain activities and progress in the light of the various conditions impinging on the teaching. It might also enhance the coherence and substance of the communications about the teaching between the experienced and the beginning teacher. There was general agreement with this view and particularly with the idea that the Conditions and their effects on standards and Teachers' Actions be a major facet of the model of teaching presented to the student.

We did not initiate the question of whether the framework of concepts might also be of value to communications among experienced teachers in, say, in-service contexts. Several teachers brought this matter up, however, and commented, for example, that: 'We never sit and talk to each other about how we teach. If we spent a lot more time finding out from each other what we did, we could solve a lot of problems and improve the teaching.'

Preparing to delve further

From the reactions of these 16 teachers, it appeared that our framework of concepts (see Figure 5.1) was acceptable to them and some found it stimulating and helpful in thinking about their own teaching. They readily recognized their own thinking when it was structured by us in accordance with our model, were not aware of it introducing any distortions and could not identify any significant inadequacies in it. Further information, elicited during discussion of the framework, seemed to fit within the same group of concepts. And while no test was made of its actual usefulness for student-teachers, or for communications between teachers, there was a generally positive reaction to the idea that it might be helpful in those circumstances. Those findings encouraged us to retain the framework at least for the time being.

We knew very little, however, about *how* the teachers did the things which they did well. We had scarcely any understanding of the mental processes underlying a teacher's routine recognition of a situation as having such-and-such characteristics, of a pupil as being such-and-such a kind of pupil, of such-and-such an action on the part of the teacher being appropriate, and so on. Although we felt we had a crude notion of what a Routine was, we had no idea of their finer structure or of the ways in which teachers used them in their teaching. We had only the sketchiest view of the extent to which Routines would turn out to be common across teachers, or across lessons. These are the kinds of matters which guided the later stages of our work described in the next chapter.

Summary

In this chapter we have, through a discussion of Conditions which impinge on teaching, completed the general framework for describing the pro-fessional craft knowledge of teaching that we have derived from the 16 teachers' accounts of their teaching. This framework was shown in Figure 5.1. We have described how five types of conditions are taken account of by teachers both in setting the standards which they seek to attain in relation to Normal Desirable States of Pupil Activity or to types of Progress and also in the Actions which they take in order to attain these goals. The five types of Conditions were those relating to: *pupils'* characteristics, including both perceived stable characteristics and more temporary ones, and both the characteristics of individuals and those of groups or whole classes; *time* Conditions, concerning the time of day or the time in the week at which a lesson was being held, or else the amount of time which the teacher had for the lesson or for making decisions; *content*, what the lesson was about, whether it was new or left over, how interesting it was for the pupils, how demanding it was, and the distinctive requirements of the particular content; *material* Conditions, including size of class, equipment available, size and layout of rooms, and weather; and finally, characterics of the *teachers* themselves, including their states of mind and body, their habits,

specific 'mistakes' they made, or their non-teaching duties. Having outlined our framework, we tentatively defined in relation to it the ideal of a
Routine, as a standardized pattern of action which a teacher undertakes. In
this chapter we have also described how we fed our understanding back to
teachers for their comments. The 'stories' which we told them explicitly
structured our interpretations of what they had said about their teaching in
terms of our framework. All of the teachers reacted positively to these
accounts, all of them appearing to find the framework satisfactory for
talking about their teaching, with several claiming that it was helpful to
them.

6

The routines teachers use to achieve their goals

Moving from the 'what' to the 'how'

In the earlier stages of our work, we were concerned with the exploration of what it was in their teaching which the teachers participating in the study saw themselves as doing well. We developed a framework (see Figure 5.1, p. 70) reflecting the kinds of criteria the teachers used in evaluating their own teaching. The teachers seemed to recognize this framework, accept it as adequate and, in some instances, find it helpful. Although we were encouraged by all this, we realized we still did not know much about how they did the things which they did well. The next phase of the research, therefore, had two aims: we wanted to investigate in greater depth the insights from the findings of the first stage, and to see if we could help the teachers make explicit how they achieved their successes in their teaching. This chapter is concerned with how we went about this and what we found.

Given the kind of detailed information we were seeking, it seemed sensible to restrict our work to collaboration with not more than 5 of the 16 teachers involved in the earlier phase of the research, and to concentrate on the secondary sector. Five teachers with specialisms in art, computing studies, English, French and physical education agreed to continue to be involved in the work. But what were we asking them to undertake?

As well as developing a framework of concepts, we had a general idea about the nature of Routines which experienced teachers use to achieve their goals. In bringing Routines into play teachers take cognizance of the Conditions impinging on their teaching and select more or less

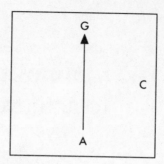

Figure 6.1   A simple Routine

automatically from their large repertoire of Actions that which is appropriate to their immediate Goal. That Goal will be either the maintenance of some Normal Desirable State of Activity (NDS) or the promotion of some kind of Progress. The simplest form for a Routine of that kind is represented in Figure 6.1 where a single Action (A) is taken under a particular set of Conditions (C) to achieve a single Goal (G).

The adequacy of the representation illustrated in Figure 6.1 was, we knew, doubtful. On the one hand, the immediacy and speed which characterizes teachers' classroom decisions would be well served by having only three major concepts. On the other hand, it was inconceivable that such a simple-minded picture could reflect the complexity of real classroom events. We moved on, therefore, to try to flesh out and unpack the concepts and their interrelationships, to investigate the patterns of Routines, and, if possible, to relate them to the teachers' mental processes as they made judgements and took actions to achieve their goals.

To provide a focus and stimulus for the teachers to discuss their teaching further, we decided to identify a set of rough and ready Routines for each teacher. At that stage we were not in a position to refine the Routines, but we knew that each must have elements of Goal, Conditions and Action. In addition, we ensured that for each teacher each Routine had been identified in several lessons, the Routines showed some variety and there was no element of ambiguity in their identification.

Examples of rough and ready Routines

So what was the nature of these Routines? As an example, one of those identified in the accounts the physical education teacher gave of his teaching reflected a Goal (NDS) which he had in most of his lessons: that pupils, recognized as reluctant to try certain physical activities, would apply themselves with effort to the activity. Several Conditions, on the same or different occasions, could work against this: pupils could be low achievers in the particular physical activity, or they might be fearful of attempting it, or they might dislike the thought of the public spectacle of taking part. The Actions which this teacher routinely brought into play to achieve his goal under the Conditions included encouraging pupils to apply themselves to the task by working hard to remove the idea that because a pupil cannot do something there is something wrong with him or her, or softening the formal instruction by introducing an element of fun, or setting a standard for a pupil which was below that for the class as a whole and ensuring that the individual achieved it.

Perhaps the most salient mark of the experienced teacher in contrast with the beginning teacher is being able to retrieve a lesson which has started to deteriorate. As a second example, one of the English teacher's Routines focused on his Goal (NDS) of recovering the pattern of class activity when things seemed not to be going well with pupils' interest and responses during the reading aloud of a text. A number of Conditions could work against such recovery: the option of abruptly moving to the next stage of the lesson might not be open because the pupils need time and familiarity with the text before they can attempt the new tasks, or pupils might resent and resist attempts to get them to put more effort into their reading and so distance themselves even more from the text. Recognizing the limitations imposed by these 'content' and 'pupil' Conditions, this teacher tended to take part himself in the reading and to identify and accentuate the humour in the text by laughing. In this way he regained the pupils' attention and helped them recognize the humorous parts.

These two examples relate to Routines with NDS Goals. Others, of course, reflect Progress Goals. The art teacher, for example, frequently articulated her Goal that pupils would produce imaginative work. Conditions which limited this kind of Progress included: pupils' lack of the technical skills which are necessary prerequisites of the imaginative work, and the tendency of some individuals to produce large, quick drawings then declare themselves finished. In response to these Conditions, the teacher might provide direct assistance with the technical aspect which is causing the problem, or might add a small amount of detail to a drawing to stimulate the pupils' own imagination.

From each teacher's accounts of their teaching in the post-lesson interviews, we were able to identify four or five Routines which turned up in several of their lessons. Our descriptions of these Routines were refined through discussion with the teachers. We are not claiming that the Routines provide a comprehensive account of how these teachers talked about their lessons; but they did reflect salient patterns which frequently emerged from that talk and, the teachers agreed, were representative of much of their classroom teaching.

Delving deeper into teachers' Routines

It was time to embark on more data collection. Once again we observed and audio-recorded lessons; this time we restricted ourselves to one per week over a period of six weeks with each teacher. Immediately following each lesson we asked the teacher whether any of the Routines which we had been discussing with him or her had occurred on that occasion, and if so at what point in the lesson. The researcher's role in the identification of these Routines was minimal for two reasons: first, our continuing concern was with the *teachers'* perceptions of their own teaching, and secondly, many of the cues for the existence of the Routines were concealed from the stranger in the classroom. How could one know, unless the teacher said so, that some pupils had pleased her by producing imaginative work, or that others were known by the teacher to be reluctant to participate? The researcher's observation task, therefore, was to keep a record of the major events of the lesson in terms of the tape-count on the audio recording. This did much to facilitate the later identification of the Routine on the audio-tape. For example, one teacher identified the management of a particularly unruly pupil as part of a Routine; the researcher's record of the lesson included all the teacher's interactions with that pupil during the lesson, and so the excerpts relevant to the Routine were relatively easily located.

We were keen to use these excerpts as an aid to teachers' recall of the Routines. Within 24 hours of the lesson we undertook a longer interview in which we played the excerpts to the teachers to help them to describe and explain their actions more fully and, perhaps, to recall the sequences of their thought processes behind these actions. This form of interviewing is called 'stimulated-recall' (cf. Calderhead 1981b).

But what were we actually asking the teachers in these interviews that we had not asked in the earlier stages? We had moved on from our previous question 'What did you think was good about your teaching?' to 'How did you achieve the things which you did well?'

One of our interests here was to enquire into the status of any particular set of Goals, Conditions and Actions in relation to the totality of their teaching. By that we mean that if, say, a teacher mentioned a particular pattern of activity as desirable, we wanted to know whether it would always be seen as desirable, or only for *particular kinds of lessons*, or only because it happened to be part of this *particular pre-lesson plan*, or only because of something which *arose on this particular occasion in the lesson*.

On the whole, this line of questioning was not fruitful. The teachers did not give any account of making mental distinctions of this kind as they came to see something as desirable. The most they might say would be something like: 'Well I wouldn't see it as appropriate to take an action like that if they were doing a test, but any other sort of lesson – OK.'

Our second main concern was to investigate how the teacher's understanding of the situation led him or her to take a particular course of action. We asked what it was about the pupils and other aspects of the situation which led the teacher to decide that action was called for, and tried further to probe the 'history' of that decision. Why did the teacher consider it appropriate to take action? Was there something from his or her experience of teaching which led to the decision that this was such-and-such a situation and that action was called for? What led to the selection of this action from other possible actions? What was it, in detail, they saw themselves as doing?

The questions clearly imply that as well as being interested in what the teachers did and why, we were also trying to get at the mental processes which prompted their assessment of, and reactions to, any given classroom situation. For the first of these objectives, we were well satisfied with what the teachers had to say. For the second, however, our success was much more limited.

All the teachers gave coherent accounts of their reasons for acting the way they did. They made sense of what they had done in retrospect and provided plenty of detailed information about the Action they took. But they did not say anything about the sequence of mental events which led them to act in the way they did, about what was in their minds at the time, about the process by which their thinking moved among Goals, Conditions and Action. As they represented it, there appeared to be a rational progression from identification of Goals through perceptions of Conditions to decisions about Action. But we have no way of knowing if those were simply rationalized reports of the real sequence of mental processes (which may well not have followed this neat linear path). We gained little insight, therefore, into how teachers select the Routines they use, and so cannot claim to have achieved access to that aspect of teachers' craft knowledge. What we can claim, however, is to have developed a better understanding of the structure of what we have called Routines and their interrelationships.

The structures of teachers' Routines

Figure 6.1 suggests the simplest form which a Routine might take with a single Goal, a given set of Conditions and pursued by a single Action. In practice, we found that the number of Goals which the teachers had was very much smaller than the number of Actions taken; the same Goal might be pursued on different occasions (and so under different Conditions) by quite different Actions; and usually the Routines were characterized by several Actions being taken to achieve one Goal; only rarely did the teachers report a single Action leading to a single Goal (as in Figure 6.1). In one such rare example, a teacher reported giving fulsome praise (Action) in

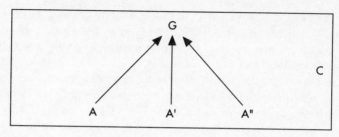

Figure 6.2   A Routine in which several Actions are taken to achieve the Goal

order that a less-able pupil (Condition) could experience public encouragement in the lesson (Goal).

The more common pattern, with multiple Actions, is illustrated (see Figure 6.2) by the teacher whose Goal (NDS) was that a reluctant pupil should be active in the work of the lesson. Conditions seen by the teacher as impinging on the teaching included her perception of the pupil as a low achiever in the subject, as being frustrated by not being able to manage things he would like to do, and as creating consequent behaviour problems when the teacher's help was not immediately forthcoming. The teacher reported taking three Actions to achieve her Goal under these Conditions. She:

- gave him something to keep him occupied while he was waiting for her to come and help him
- gave him the technical assistance he was seeking
- suggested an alternative idea when pointing out to him that one of his ideas would not work.

As we have already suggested, it was not unusual for teachers to have the same Goal in several lessons. If the Conditions were different, the Actions taken would be different and so we would conclude that these were different routines, but related because of being characterized by the same Goal. The teacher mentioned in the last example had the same Goal (that a reluc-

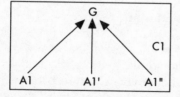
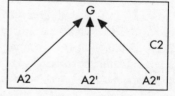

Figure 6.3   Routines on different occasions, under different Conditions, where different Actions are taken to achieve the same Goal

Goal: Pupils within a group will work well together	
Lesson 1 Conditions 1 • Group members never work well together. • One member easily bored. • One needs a lot of teacher's attention. • One new to the school. Actions 1 The teacher: • tells group to remove outdoor gear • spends a lot of time with them to keep them at their work • keeps them in his line of vision while with other groups.	Lesson 2 Conditions 2 • Group pays too much attention to a neighbouring group. • Group lacks a dominant individual to coordinate their efforts. • Worksheets in use need some alteration. Actions 2 The teacher: • asks the group questions they cannot answer to point out they are not reading the instructions • gives them help and encouragement.

Figure 6.4   Two Routines with the same Goal but different Conditions and so different Actions

tant pupil should be active) in the following lesson. In this case, however, it was a different pupil and the new Conditions perceived by the teacher were of a lazy pupil but one presenting no problems of discipline. She described her Actions as:

• refraining from asking him to finish off another exercise before continuing with the one he was on
• giving him the technical assistance he was seeking
• refraining from suggesting a more elaborate approach to solving his difficulty.

An interesting feature of these Actions is the inclusion of 'avoidance' actions. These played an important part in teachers' accounts of their Routines. This pair of related Routines are represented by Figure 6.3. Figure 6.4 provides another example of two Routines from one teacher showing the same goal. These examples demonstrate clearly how the teachers' perceptions of differing Conditions lead to quite distinctive choices of Action.

In each of these Routines it appeared that the Actions were mutually reinforcing and taken in parallel (or at any rate in no particular order) to achieve the Goal. This was a common feature of the teachers' reports. For example, one teacher with the Goal that pupils would understand what they had to do, took Action which:

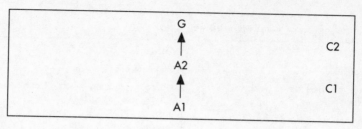

Figure 6.5 A Routine with sequential Actions where the first Action changes the Condition

- avoided using difficult terms, which were new to the pupils
- kept his language simple
- used the example of the long jump to point out the difference of the actions of the high jump.

Another, whose Goal was the control of a potentially disruptive pupil while remaining approachable to that pupil:

- ignored the pupil's attempts at provocation
- told the pupil she would be praised when her work was good, but rebuked when it was poor, or she behaved badly
- reacted to her work as if nothing untoward was happening in the lesson
- replied in the negative to her request for a rest.

The second of these demonstrates an interesting point which we will return to later: the teacher is stating two Goals here so there are two Routines with different Goals but a shared set of Conditions and Actions.

In another case of multiple Actions to achieve a Goal, the Actions were undertaken sequentially rather than in parallel. Sometimes that was because one Action seemed to be dependent on the 'successful' outcome of a prior Action; for example, a teacher might first make sure that all the pupils were looking at her and only then start speaking. Figure 6.5 represents this sequential relationship; it indicates that the Conditions may change as a result of the first Action (in the example above the pupils are no longer inattentive). The illustrations of this included one teacher who with the Goal of an indisciplined pupil doing some work:

- gave the pupil a warning about his behaviour
- then gave him help when he sought it
- then moved him to another part of the room when his behaviour did not improve.

In another lesson the same teacher, wishing to control a different badly-behaved pupil but at the same time endeavouring to maintain a good relationship with him:

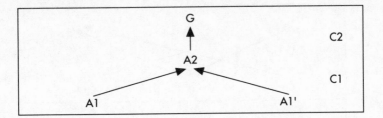

Figure 6.6   A Routine where the Actions are taken both in parallel and sequentially

- gave the pupil a warning about his behaviour
- then, as the disruption continued, told him quietly to come back at the end of the day
- then, since things failed to improve, told the pupil to move to another seat
- and finally, announced to the class at the end of the lesson that the pupil was to return at the end of the day.

Most frequently, however, we found a combination of parallel *and* sequentially related Actions (see Figure 6.6). For example, a teacher whose Goal was to achieve a good work rate from pupils:

- went over the work of the previous week
- introduced new activities
- used his tone of voice to accentuate key points
- had a quick turnover of activities
- circulated the pupil groups to keep them at the activities
- used a pupil to help him demonstrate an action
- used a pupil to comment on the performance of a group
- praised a pupil to the class.

Although we have presented the teachers' knowledge as primarily concerned with the Actions necessary to achieve one specific Goal in a given set of Conditions, we have already suggested that teachers are some-times concerned to attain more than one Goal contemporaneously using the same set of Actions (see Figure 6.7). In an example similar to the one already cited, a teacher directed his Actions towards the correction of a pupil's breach of discipline while at the same time endeavouring to main-tain an image of himself as approachable. He took a sequence of Actions in which he:

- told the pupil to return to her seat
- told her again, this time in a mock 'aghast' tone
- made an exaggerated comment about the mayhem of the class in general, while mopping his brow elaborately.

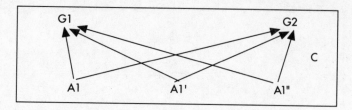

Figure 6.7 A Routine in which the same set of Actions are taken to achieve two distinctive Goals

Sometimes the multiple Goals were all 'positive'; so, for example, one teacher aimed for the pupils to understand what they were doing rather than just following her directions, *and* for them to enjoy the lesson. Frequently, however, one of the Goals was an 'avoidance' of undesirable states or events. Another teacher, for instance, was concerned that all the pupils should have sufficient time to understand the work of the lesson, but also placed substantial emphasis on the importance of avoiding the more able pupils becoming bored.

It is not necessarily the case, of course, that two Goals will be achieved by one set of Actions. In some cases, the teacher may adopt separate sets of Actions to achieve each Goal and these Actions may be mutually compatible (see Figure 6.8). So, for example, one teacher's main Goal was that the pupils should attend to the lesson content throughout. To this end he:

- told the class what they had to do
- told them to work quietly
- acceded to a pupil request to play a tape
- laid out work of his own on a group desk so that the talkative members of the group had to sit at individual desks.

At the same time, however, he was anxious to improve relations with a pupil who had been in trouble on the previous day. To achieve this he:

- offered to help with her work
- passed a lighthearted conversation with her.

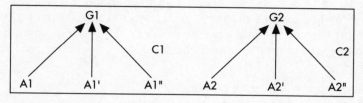

Figure 6.8 Two concurrent Routines with two compatible sets of Actions to achieve two Goals

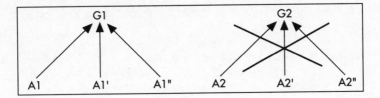

Figure 6.9   Two concurrent Routines in which the Actions to achieve one Goal are incompatible with those to achieve the other

In the cases above, the achievement of one of the Goals does not have to be at the expense of the other. Sometimes, however, the actions to achieve the different Goals may be incompatible and choices have to be made (see Figure 6.9). It seems that teachers then adopt the Routine directed towards the more highly valued Goal. If they have the option, they will choose Actions which least endanger their other Goals. One teacher, for example, was particularly concerned that an individual pupil should have the confidence to seek the teacher's help when she needed it. However, a further aim was that the pupil should not copy ideas. In achieving her first Goal, the teacher encouraged, helped and responded positively to requests and suggestions from the pupil. But because the main suggestion put forward by the pupil involved copying something, the teacher decided to abandon the pursuit of her second Goal in favour of the first.

Although we have identified a number of different ways in which the Routines teachers use are structured, our small samples of teachers and of their talk about teaching prevents us from estimating the frequency of occurrence of the alternatives. Table 6.1 indicates the number of teachers, from our sample of five, who described each characteristic Routine pattern to us.

The variety of the possible structures of Routines was not unexpected. We commented at the start of this chapter that the limited number of general concepts (Goals, Conditions and Actions) seemed consistent with the demands for immediacy and speed of classroom decisions. A teacher who stands in front of a class, systematically searching through a plethora of concepts and theories of teaching, is likely to find the class has deteriorated into turmoil, or left, before a decision is made. On the other hand, it is obvious that teaching is not just a simple business of deciding on a Goal and picking the right Action to achieve it. The complicated nature of teaching decisions comes about because there are a large number of different Goals which teachers have, a virtually infinite variety of combinations of Conditions impinging on teaching and a vast array of possible Actions from which to choose. Whether we have chosen wisely in deciding to describe the combinations of these in the practice of teaching 'Routines' we are in some doubt. In common with what is usually thought of as routine

Table 6.1 The number of teachers who described each type of Routine
(five teachers involved)

Characteristics of the Routine	No. of teachers	Reference figure in text
1 Only one Action to achieve Goal	1	6.1
2 Compatible Actions taken in parallel to achieve a Goal	5	6.2
3 Routines with same Goal, in different lessons, different Conditions and Actions	5	6.3 and 6.4
4 Actions taken in sequence to achieve a Goal	3	6.5
5 Mixture of parallel and sequential Actions to achieve Goal	4	6.6
6 More than one Goal pursued by the same set of Actions	2	6.7
7 More than one Goal pursued by different but compatible sets of Actions	1	6.8
8 Competing Goals with non-compatible Actions where one Goal threatened	3	6.9

activities, they are spontaneous and largely automatic, but in their
complexity they are quite different.

The substance of teachers' Goals and Conditions

Our analysis by this time convinced us that the general concepts which we
developed in the earlier work, described in Chapters 4 and 5, were still
appropriate in the more detailed study. Furthermore, those concepts had
enabled us to examine in some detail what we had called Routines which
the teachers use in achieving their goals. Our final questions concerned the
content of what the teachers were saying. To what extent were they all
talking about the same Goals? Were the kinds of Goals they mentioned
different from those identified in the first stage of the research involving
more teachers? Were the kinds of Conditions we had identified in the
earlier work still standing up, and had the teachers anything to add to that
list?

Even though we had identified only four or five Routines for each teacher, there was clear evidence of some common Goals. Comparisons showed repeated evidence for the emphasis on maintaining patterns of classroom activity (NDS), and of shared aspirations for:

- A good and easy relationship between the teacher and pupils in the classroom.
- Pupils to be understanding what the teacher is asking them to do.
- Pupils who (for whatever reason) are reluctant to work, to be actually working.
- *All* pupils to be applying themselves well to the work.
- Pupils to be thinking about, and understanding, what they are doing, rather than just doing what they are told.

Individual teachers also had distinctive priorities for the Normal Desirable States of activity in their classrooms. The art teacher, for example, laid great emphasis on pupils continually making use of their imaginations, and on effective organization of the diverse classroom activities to suit the differences among individual pupils. In contrast, the computing studies teacher stressed the importance of keeping pupils working well together as a group, and of the activities following a structured sequence through the lesson. To what extent these reflect subject differences rather than differences between individual teachers we cannot say. Our sample is clearly too small to make such a distinction.

The more detailed exploration of the basis on which teachers choose to take particular actions to achieve their activity goals, confirmed the importance they attach to the various categories of Conditions impinging on their teaching. The most frequently mentioned Conditions related to pupils. In some cases, teachers were basing their judgements proactively on their perceptions of individual pupils' generalizable limitations: short attention span, unlikely to understand, cannot be relied upon to remember. In other cases, behavioural indicators such as signs of pupils not understanding, not having heard, not having remembered or misbehaving were the cues which teachers reacted to and acted upon. One aspect of pupil Conditions which emerged with more salience in this later stage of the research might be described as the stereotyping of pupil *groups*. Assumed characteristics of, say, first year groups or high ability groups influenced teachers' Actions, even if behaviour relevant to those characteristics was not apparent.

There was, however, another factor which bore upon the judgements teachers made about how they should act, and our earlier framework did not take this into account. This arose from the multiple goals which the teachers always had in mind. For example, in explaining how they came to take a set of Actions they would remind us that they always aim to be seen by pupils to be acting 'fairly', or to behave in a way that takes into account relationships between pupils, or to avoid the appearance of having lost control of the situation. We have already suggested that sometimes teachers have goals which are incompatible and so one or more has to be abandoned. It appeared that the teachers were faced quite frequently with goals which apparently were in conflict and this had to be resolved in some way. They often talked about the balance which must be kept between, for example:

- Encouraging the shy pupils and dampening down the boisterous.
- Giving the slow workers time to finish and avoiding the fast workers becoming bored.
- Stretching the high achievers, and avoiding the low achievers becoming demoralized.
- Maintaining a friendly classroom atmosphere, but retaining the authority of the teacher.

All this makes us even more aware that we have broken into just a small corner of teachers' professional craft knowledge. But we have done enough to convince ourselves that teachers have a great deal of rich and valuable information to pass on to us, to student-teachers and to other experienced teachers. How to provide the conditions which will persuade teachers to share their expertise and allow all these groups to have access to the knowledge is a priority task for the future.

Other perspectives on the classroom: observers' and pupils'

We have put a great deal of emphasis on the importance and value of teachers' articulation of their own professional craft knowledge. Before moving on to the conclusions and implications arising from this research, however, it is worth briefly commenting on the perspectives of the others who were present when the teaching was taking place, i.e. ourselves as observers and the pupils. The main function of collecting data from these two sources was, as we have explained, to encourage the teachers to give us the information we were seeking. But the same kinds of data could be used to explore the question of how adequate an understanding of what teachers are doing in classrooms can be gleaned from the judgements of observers or pupils. Although this question was not the focus of the research reported in this book, it is crucial (as we suggested in Chapter 1) that it be addressed in any rational planning for observation of teaching as part of appraisal.

An examination of our (outsiders') observations of teaching, carried out *before* the teachers were given the opportunity to explain to us what they were doing, showed that our procedures served our research well. However, it also illustrated the shortcomings of observation, even when it is well informed, as the sole basis of judgements about classroom teaching.

Our observations, not surprisingly, reflected the ways in which *we* construed the teaching and these were not necessarily salient for the teacher.
Furthermore, in comparison with the teachers' accounts of the lessons,
it was clear that the observers' reports were often superficial and lacking
the richness which comes with established knowledge about the pupils
and the other conditions impinging on the teaching. Where the observations *followed* discussions with the teacher about what he or she was
trying to do, there was a better opportunity to focus on, and elaborate, those
interrelated facets of the teaching which gave it coherence within the
teachers' own framework. As researchers our task was to analyse, not to
evaluate, but our findings suggest that an evaluator who bases judgements
on observation alone, without teachers' explanations of what they are
doing, will do so on an inadequate understanding, or even a misunder-
standing, of what is going on in the classroom.

Turning to the data collected from pupils, it is of interest to know how
their perceptions compare with those of the teachers. Batten (1989: 56)
undertook a comparison, using our data, of the teachers' and pupils'
accounts of the same set of classroom events and provided an analysis of
the similarities and differences in the views expressed about the positive
aspects of the teaching. She concluded:

> the aspects of teaching that were identified by teachers and pupils
> were concerned not only with teaching strategies, as anticipated, but
> also with pupil outcomes (particularly in the case of teachers) and
> classroom and lesson management (particularly in the case of pupils);
> 17 comment categories were common to both groups and 12 cate-
> gories were identified by one group only.
>
> Nearly all of the most frequent comments were in the common
> categories of the classification, indicating some agreement between
> teachers and pupils. Both groups agreed on the importance of
> teacher help and encouragement, and pupil interest and enjoyment.
> Differences in priorities were seen in the emphasis given by teachers
> to learning acquisition and pupil participation on the one hand, and
> the strong emphasis given by pupils to explanation and instruction on
> the other.
>
> Teachers' comments were more detailed and complex than those
> of the pupils and were concerned with before and after as well as
> the lesson itself, whereas pupils tended to respond only to activities
> within the lesson. This finding was not unexpected, given that the
> training and professional responsibility of teachers induces a broader
> vision of a lesson, incorporating purposes and outcomes.

Teachers and pupils sometimes identified the same positive aspects of a
particular lesson, but this was by no means always the case and often the
emphasis on a particular aspect was different for teacher and pupils.

One particularly interesting finding from this analysis was the frequency with which pupils, but not teachers, referred to the good explanations and clear instructions provided. Attention has been drawn elsewhere to the importance of explanation as a component of effective teaching (e.g. Roehler and Duffy 1986), and Batten (1989: 57) argues that the perceptiveness of pupils in this area is a valuable contribution to our understanding of teaching:

> Brown and McIntyre (1988: 45) concluded, after a detailed examination of teachers' lesson commentaries, that the major concern of the teachers was to maintain normal desirable states of pupil activity and to promote pupil progress; their own actions were only mentioned in relation to these pupil-focused goals. The present study showed that pupils were able to identify quite specifically those actions of the teacher which contributed to a successful lesson.

Summary

In this chapter, we have described an extended study which we conducted into how five of the teachers studied earlier did the things they did well. For each of these teachers we identified from the earlier work a number of 'routines' which they used frequently, i.e. goals which they regularly sought using actions chosen from their repertoires according to the prevailing conditions. With a high degree of consistency we found the teachers unable to report to us the mental processes involved in their classroom decision-making. They were able to give us, however, a fuller picture than previously of what they did and why. Thus it turned out that these teachers rarely took single actions to attain single goals. We have reported in this chapter the various ways in which combinations of actions, sequential or concurrent or both, chosen according to diverse conditions, are used to attain one goal or possibly more than one goal; and we have reported some circumstances in which the actions which teachers found necessary for attaining two different concurrent goals were mutually incompatible, so that the teachers were obliged to concentrate on their more important goals. The different combinations of goals, actions and conditions which teachers face in the course of every lesson led us to question our use of the term 'routine', although the speed, fluency and apparent lack of deliberation involved in these teacher activities were compatible with such a description. Towards the end of the chapter we raised the questions of how far teachers share the same goals, repertoires of actions and conditions attended to, and of how much observers' and pupils' perceptions of classroom events can add to teachers' own accounts.

7

Making sense of teaching: conclusions and implications

We set out in this investigation to try to understand better the nature of teaching in schools, and in particular to understand teaching from the perspective of the people doing it – the teachers. We recognized that this was a difficult task, because it seemed clear that experienced teachers' effectiveness was dependent on a fluency of action which would be possible only if the action was spontaneous, largely automatic, and based on only very limited conscious examination of available options. That being so, we did not know whether teachers would be able to explain to us what they had been doing in their teaching or why they had done these things. Furthermore, we were anxious not to lead teachers into describing or explaining their teaching in terms of our presuppositions, nor to encourage them to talk about their teaching in terms of 'espoused theories' (Schön 1983) which did not reflect the ways they actually thought in classrooms.

In this final chapter we reflect first on the extent to which we have been successful in achieving access to the thinking that underlies what teachers do in classrooms and second on the new understandings of that thinking which we have achieved. We then go on to consider the implications of these new understandings for the several practical problems which, as we explained in Chapter 1, led us to undertake this investigation. Finally, and properly, we focus on some of the many questions which remain unanswered but which as a result of this investigation may be seen to be worthy of research attention.

The possibility of gaining access to teachers' professional craft knowledge

How can one discover the knowledge and thoughts which underlie the actions of a person who is engaged in a complex interaction with others? We came to the conclusion that the only possible way of doing this, if we were not to make too many questionable assumptions, was by asking the person concerned, as soon as possible afterwards, to tell us what underlay his or her actions; and that was the method we used to gather our evidence. That, however, left us with a problem: if we were right in believing we had used the only possible way, how could we check on the validity of our findings? There was no alternative source from which we could obtain evidence against which our findings could be tested.

It seems to us to be impossible in principle to be certain about whether or not we have successfully gained access to teachers' professional craft knowledge. We are none the less very confident that we did so.

This confidence is based to some extent on the teachers' own consistency in their accounts of their teaching: what they said when commenting on tape-recorded extracts from units was not significantly different in form or substance from what they had said after particular lessons; when they were later presented with our accounts of what they had said, they enthusiastically endorsed these as valid representations of the thinking underlying their teaching; and the five teachers whose teaching and thinking we explored more fully talked of their teaching on successive occasions in the same kind of way. Finally, virtually everything that all the teachers said on all occasions could be represented in terms of the models which we abstracted. Thus we had good reason to be confident about the validity of our descriptions of these 16 teachers' articulation of their professional craft knowledge.

To some extent also our confidence is based on the face validity of our results. To us the teachers' accounts have seemed consistently rich, relevant, focused and persuasive; and having presented these results to some hundreds of teachers and researchers on teaching, we have found a very general readiness to accept them as plausible and sensible. Nobody has suggested to us that the teachers were approaching their teaching in unusual ways or that their reported thinking seemed improbable.

Our confidence is based mainly, however, on the belief that conditions were created in which the teachers were both able and willing to recall the thinking which underlay their actions. Because of our strong emphasis on what had been successful in their teaching, they had no reason to be defensive and instead gave every appearance of trying hard to articulate their perceptions of their successes and what had been involved in their achievement. Because the researcher had always observed the particular events under discussion, there was both an opportunity to concentrate on these particular occasions and an obligation to give accounts consonant with what had happened on these occasions; and this the teachers consistently did. Because the researcher did not introduce any ideas which might be used in describing or explaining what had happened, the teachers were entirely dependent on their individual ways of construing the events of the observed lessons. Because the main interviews were conducted very soon after the observed lessons, it was probable that the teachers would be able to recall their thinking during the lessons, and they themselves claimed to be able to do so. Because they were asked to articulate that recalled thinking orally, their preferred mode, opportunities for introducing ideas which were not already in the forefront of their minds were reduced. Thus although we cannot demonstrate the validity of our claim to have gained access to teachers' professional craft knowledge, we believe that these various characteristics of the processes by which teachers' accounts were generated justify the confidence with which we make that claim.

That said, we must be clear about what it is that we are claiming. We can make no claims to have discovered anything about the *processes* of teachers' classroom thinking. The teachers revealed to us a great deal about what they saw themselves as having successfully achieved in their lessons, about how they achieved these things, and about factors that influenced the standards they set and the means they chose. Thus they were able to recall the *conclusions* of their classroom thinking about what to do, and how, and why. We had also been interested in how they came to these conclusions: for example, how were they first alerted to the need to take action? What information did they seek about the situations that faced them? How did they use the information available to them? In general, however, they were unable to give us access to such information. They seemed able to remember quite fluently what they had thought about classroom situations, but they could not recall their own mental processes. Not surprisingly, interactive teaching seems to be too demanding for teachers to be able to devote any attention to monitoring their own mental activities. It is then the substance and the logic of the professional craft knowledge used by teachers that we can describe, not the psychology of their thinking.

To be able to conclude that we have gained access to the substance and logic of teachers' professional craft knowledge is to us of major importance. If this conclusion had not been justified, we should have been at a loss to know how access could be gained. We should indeed have been forced to question the possibility of access. But having concluded that access to teachers' professional craft knowledge *is* possible, we believe that it will be necessary for this knowledge to be explored much more fully and widely, and for the recognition of this knowledge to be given central importance in

policy-making on teachers' professional education and development,
curriculum planning, teacher appraisal, teachers' conditions and effective
schooling.

The nature of teachers' professional craft knowledge: general findings

Any conclusions which we reach on the nature of teachers' professional
craft knowledge must of course be very tentative since these conclusions
are based on the study of 16 carefully selected teachers, with classes in the
10 to 14 age range, in one city comprehensive school and its feeder primary
schools. While we are confident of some generalized conclusions across
these 16 teachers, we have no firm basis for any generalizations beyond this
small sample.

Furthermore, it seems highly likely that our findings reflected to a considerable degree the approach which we took to exploring professional
craft knowledge. For example, we observed and asked questions about the
lessons themselves, not about the preparation for these lessons. Also, we
undertook the study in a cross-curricular way, clearly not as specialists in
the various subjects being taught (nor indeed as specialists in the primary
age range). These factors may well have led to the relative lack of emphasis
in the teachers' accounts on the particular subject topics they were teaching and on their attempts to facilitate learning related to these specific
topics – what Shulman (1986) calls 'pedagogical content knowledge'.

Another significant aspect of our approach was the adoption, as a framework within which professional craft knowledge was explored, of teachers'
perceptions of what had been successful in their lessons. Craft knowledge
of a rather different kind might possibly have been revealed if the focus had
been on teachers' *problems* in their teaching. Or again, it seems likely that
teachers routinely achieve a great deal which they so take for granted as
not even to notice; and the craft knowledge implicit in these more taken-
for-granted achievements may also be rather different in kind. We make no
claims, therefore, about the *comprehensiveness* of the professional craft
knowledge revealed to us, even in relation to the kinds of craft knowledge
used by the 16 teachers with whom we worked. None the less, these 16
teachers revealed to us, in a wide variety of lessons, professional craft
knowledge in which some strongly pervasive patterns were apparent.

What then have we discovered about teachers' professional craft knowledge as it relates to what the teachers recognized themselves as having
done well?

One important generalization is that the teachers most commonly judged
their teaching in terms of the achievement or maintenance of states of
pupil activity which they took to be normally desirable for particular phases

and types of lesson (NDS). Each teacher appeared to have his or her own characterisation of the kind of pupil activity appropriate for each of a small number of kinds of lesson and for each major phase of these lessons. It is not possible of course to say from our evidence to what extent perceptions of NDS are, for example, shared by teachers of the same subject or differentiated according to pupil age groups.

Success was also perceived sometimes when some kind of Progress was apparent in pupils' confidence, attitudes, understanding or skills, in the completion of artefacts, in coverage of the work, or towards an NDS of activity. Notable for its absence was any suggestion that teachers' success could be judged simply in terms of the quality of what they did: their lucidity in explaining, the humour of their acting, their sensitivity to pupil needs, or the enthusiasm with which a subject was projected was never in itself a cause for positive evaluation. There were few cases too, whether for single lessons or for the longer teaching units, of success being claimed because learning objectives had been attained. Most of the time, the teachers judged their own success in relation to their clear criteria for whether or not their pupils were working appropriately for a perceived stage of a perceived type of lesson.

A second important generalization is that the teachers generally had considerable repertoires of tactics which they could use in order to attain their short-term goals. What teachers did depended first on the goals (i.e. the normal desirable states or kinds of progress) that they were seeking to attain; but they chose from their repertoires those Actions which they considered appropriate in view of the specific situations in which they found themselves.

The ways in which teachers construed the situations in which they were acting were thus of central importance for their successful teaching. Among the most salient characteristics of these situations were the perceived abilities, attitudes, personalities, social skills, moods, feelings, classroom behaviour and reputations of the pupils involved. Other important Conditions included the amount of time available, the time of the day or week, the subject matter, available resources, and the teacher's own state of mind and body. Actions taken by teachers to attain short-term goals were typically chosen in the light of several such Conditions.

While the Actions which teachers took always depended on such various Conditions over which teachers had little or no control, the kinds of goals they tried to attain did not appear to depend on such Conditions but rather on the kind of lesson or the phase of the lesson. However, for any given NDS of pupil activity or type of Progress, the standards which satisfied teachers were clearly dependent on the same range of factors as those which influenced their choice of Actions.

In the final stage of our investigation, where we looked more intensively at the professional craft knowledge of five of the teachers, it became apparent that typically there were complex patterns of interdependence among Goals and Actions. Only very rarely did teachers have single Goals in mind and single tactics for attaining them. Actions would instead be chosen with several Goals in mind, and several Actions might be undertaken with the same Goal in mind. Goals, and therefore the Actions to attain them, might be dependent one on another, or mutually compatible, or in conflict. Not only, then, were teachers choosing Actions from extensive repertoires in view of a large number of possible Conditions; they were also choosing various kinds of combinations of actions to attain various kinds of combinations of Goals.

Two kinds of comment seem necessary about these general findings and the models of teachers' professional craft knowledge which we have developed. First, these findings and models are highly abstract and arid in comparison to the vital reality of the instances of professional craft knowledge in use from which they were derived. They are indeed so abstract and general that their practical value must be limited. On the other hand, it is perhaps surprising that we have been able to establish such findings which both are generalizable across 16 very different teachers and also make significant statements about the nature of professional craft knowledge. That such generalizations are possible across such diverse teachers and teaching situations gives us great confidence that very rich and practically useful generalizations will be possible when similar studies are conducted focusing on, for example, practical laboratory teaching in science, or the teaching of plays in English.

The second comment relates to the way we have ourselves conceptualized the kind of professional craft knowledge of teachers to which we have sought and gained access. Believing that teachers' classroom fluency is necessarily dependent on a large measure of routinization in their teaching, we saw ourselves as seeking access to teacher routines, and we came to define a Routine as:

> a standardized pattern of teacher action undertaken under certain recognized conditions in order to maintain a particular desired state of pupil activity or to promote a specific type of progress.

The complexity of the professional craft knowledge which we have examined leads us to be uncertain as to how 'routinized' or 'standardized' the patterns of teacher action can be. Certainly, teachers do not have time to reflect in their classrooms upon the choices open to them, and they very rarely articulate the kinds of thinking they have revealed in this study; but it seems implausible that such complex consideration of conditions, selection from repertoires, and combination of goals and actions should be describable as routine. We leave this as an issue deserving more reflection and more research.

Implications for pre-service professional education

In relation to initial teacher education, the most important and obvious conclusion to be drawn from this study is that there is a vast reservoir of experienced teachers' sophisticated professional craft knowledge which is, at least in principle, accessible to student-teachers. Yet, as we argued in Chapter 1, this reservoir of professional knowledge is generally untapped, so that beginning teachers to a very large extent have to learn their craft by trial and error from their own experience.

There are, however, other implications. The professional craft knowledge which teachers have revealed to us is highly complex, providing no simple generalizations about how to do anything well in teaching. In contrast, student-teachers tend to be anxious to find such 'recipes' for successful teaching, and indeed need to learn much simpler tactics, and to rely much more heavily on carefully planned lessons, before they can develop the fluency necessary for using the kind of professional craft knowledge that we have found experienced teachers using. Student-teachers would not, therefore, be able to make direct and immediate use of most of the professional craft knowledge which they could learn from experienced teachers. Nor indeed would it be desirable for student-teachers to imitate wholesale the individual experienced teachers with whom they happen to work.

What then would be the point of student-teachers gaining access to the professional craft knowledge of experienced teachers? The main purpose, and a very important one, we believe, would be to learn the nature of the craft they were trying to master. Without a clear conception of what one is trying to learn, one's learning must always be inefficient. Furthermore, without a clear idea of what one is learning, one's developing skills remain inaccessible to one's conscious examination, so that the values they imply, the goals to which they are directed, and the theoretical rationales which could inform them remain unquestioned and unused. On the other hand, student-teachers with a good understanding of the kind of professional craft knowledge they needed would be well placed to direct their own learning in an efficient manner and at an appropriate pace.

Continued research into teachers' professional craft knowledge should, we hope, make it increasingly possible for student-teachers to gain an extended theoretical understanding of its general nature, and of its substance in relation to particular aspects of teaching, from reading and academic study. Such study would, however, have to be complemented by access to the professional craft knowledge used by teachers working in the context in which the student-teacher was learning. This would be necessary both to exemplify the research-based generalizations and also to test them against the realities of the particular context.

How then might student-teachers gain access to the professional craft knowledge of the experienced teachers with whom they work? Our best suggestion is that so far as possible they should follow the successful procedures adopted in this research project. That however would not be easy. Student-teachers would have neither the status nor the time to set the scene as we did. It would, furthermore, be unreasonable to expect them to have the understanding, motivation, skill or self-discipline to seek access to teachers' craft knowledge as we did. More of the responsibility would have to lie with the experienced teachers, so that student-teachers' access to these teachers' craft knowledge would depend on their understanding, motivation and self-discipline. As always in schools, the enterprise would depend on the availability of time for it, and on a sufficiently high priority being given to it. Whether or not it is realistic to hope that these conditions could be met, or alternative means found for student-teachers to gain access to experienced teachers' craft knowledge, are issues which we are currently investigating. If current moves towards more school-based forms of initial teacher education are to make any sense, it will be because much greater weight is to be given to the learning of experienced teachers' professional craft knowledge; but we have only just begun to explore how this might be done. (For a report on the early stages of this research see McAlpine *et al*. 1988.)

Implications for in-service professional education

As we suggested in Chapter 1, in-service teacher education has generally been built on a 'deficit model' of teaching, aimed at overcoming teachers' perceived weaknesses. The major legitimate complaint against such an approach is not that it is insufficiently respectful of teachers but rather that it seems calculated to be ineffective. An emphasis on their inadequacies is not likely to encourage teachers to new possibilities; and procedures for developing teachers' expertise which do not involve identifying and building upon these teachers' existing strengths must at best be very inefficient.

The deficit approach to in-service education has several negative consequences. First, it makes it difficult for teachers to recognize their own skilfulness or therefore to believe that they have valuable expertise which could usefully be shared with others. Secondly, it discourages teachers from considering their own teaching analytically because they expect such analysis to be a depressing experience. Thirdly, it leads teachers defensively to close their classroom doors and to be reluctant to be observed by colleagues, in the expectation that their perceptions would be critical. This is often a valid expectation because, fourthly, the teaching profession appears very widely to have internalized this deficit view of itself, so that in their observation of one another teachers often *are* hypercritical.

We believe that our procedures and our findings offer one possible way in which these negative patterns could be reversed and a more productive approach to in-service teacher education might be developed. Most fundamentally, we have been struck by the great pleasure which teachers have obviously gained from the feedback we were able to give them about pupils' views of their strengths, and also by the satisfaction they gained from the gradual recognition that their own teaching practices involved perceptive insights, complex thinking and sophisticated judgements which they usually took for granted. We are sure that a productive way to open teachers' classroom doors to one another is through observers firmly committing themselves both to an exclusively positive view of what they observe and to understanding events from the perspective of the observed teacher. The first important and necessary benefit of such an approach is its effect on the morale of observed teachers and on their readiness to be observed on other occasions.

There are, in addition, two other major benefits. It is apparent that teachers' repertoires for achieving their goals are both rich and diverse, as are their ways of taking account of factors which impinge on classroom activities. There is thus every reason to believe that all experienced teachers can gain through a sharing of their expertise with one another. This might be done with various organizational arrangements, for example either within subject or age-range specialisms or across these boundaries, and either in an open-ended exploratory way or with a deliberate intent to learn about a specific strength of the observed teacher's teaching.

The benefits of such attempted sharing of expertise are likely to be realized only if an exclusively positive perspective is taken on the observed teaching and if time is set aside and used for post-observation discussion of the observed teacher's thinking. Teachers observed in this way do however, in our experience, tend to become much less defensive about their teaching. Instead, having begun to make their craft knowledge explicit, they are encouraged and enabled to subject that knowledge to critical examination. Teachers' recognition and sharing of their knowledge is thus not only valuable in itself but also potentially a first stage, though a necessary one for many, towards a self-critical process of professional development in which they themselves may decide to use colleagues or other observers for other kinds of observation, for example in collecting evidence on aspects of their teaching which they wish to improve.

Implications for curriculum innovation

In Chapter 1 we noted the very poor level of success that has been achieved over the years in the classroom implementation of apparently

valuable innovative educational ideas. We suggested that 'the major constraint on the acceptance of innovations by teachers is their perceived
impracticality' and that 'to have any chance of being perceived as practical,
plans for innovation would have to take account of what is already being
done (particularly what is being done well) in classrooms'. One of the aims
of this research was therefore to understand ways in which curriculum
innovators would have to take account of 'what is already being done well
in classrooms.'

From what we have found, it is at least possible to illustrate some of
the problems involved in the classroom implementation of intended
innovations. Many innovations are concerned with pupils' ways of working
in classrooms, such as the nature of their talk, their practical activity, the
sources of information they use, the ways they collaborate, the questions
they seek to answer. Such innovations seek, in our terms, to define new
'normal desirable states of pupil activity'. Some of these are likely to be
simply incompatible in their specifications of what is desirable with normal
desirable states which many teachers have learned to take for granted. In
such cases, the teachers will have to be persuaded that the newly suggested
normal desirable state is educationally superior to that which it would
replace, and that it is an achievable state of affairs in classrooms without
unreasonable efforts, and also that it would bring with it no seriously undesirable side effects. For the innovation to be 'practical', however, it would
have to be so clearly superior to the established practices, and so certainly
achievable and safe, as to justify the abandonment of the extensive repertoire of teacher tactics, and the even more extensive craft knowledge about
when to use what tactics, that each teacher had built up over the years.
Those tactics have been designed to maintain normal desirable states of
pupil activity which are now to be rejected as relatively valueless and to be
replaced by the new normal desirable state for which the teacher might
have no craft knowledge at all.

Innovative normal desirable states may not, however, be incompatible
with those which teachers take for granted. None the less, if they are
innovative at all, they will set new classroom goals for teachers, to be
attained at the same time as they work towards their more established
goals. That teachers are accustomed to taking action designed to attain
different goals simultaneously is clear from our research. It is also clear,
however, that doing this severely restricts selection from the set of actions
which might have been taken to achieve either one of them on its own.
Thus even when they have come to terms with such innovations, teachers'
use of their established repertoires will be severely constrained. If these
limitations are too severe in comparison with the perceived benefits of the
innovation, then that innovation will be seen as 'impractical'.

Other innovations may be concerned not with teachers' goals but with the ways they take account of different aspects of the situations with which they have to deal. Many innovations are concerned with teachers' use of accommodation, or resources, or time, with the ways they treat their subject matter, or the ways in which they deal with different pupils. They are concerned, then, with what we have described as 'conditions of teaching' which are important in determining the particular actions which teachers take and also the standards which they set. Considering the most important category of conditions, pupil characteristics, many important innovations are concerned with ways of thinking about and dealing with similarities and differences among pupils. For example, an innovation might be concerned with catering for pupils according to their styles of learning, or their alternative understandings of subject concepts, or simply the knowledge that they have previously mastered. If, however, as seems frequently to be the case, teachers' classroom thinking and practices were heavily dependent on descriptions of pupils in terms of their general ability at the subject, acceptance of any one of these alternative conceptualizations would probably be disabling for teachers.

We knew from the start that classroom implementation of curriculum innovations is often severely limited by teachers' perceptions of their lack of practicality. What we have discovered about teachers' professional craft knowledge enables us to understand better the nature of the constraints upon teachers' acceptance and implementation of innovations that are imposed by their reasonable expectation of not abandoning as useless important knowledge and skills which they have developed during their professional careers.

As educators, teachers frequently recognize the merits of proposed innovations; and, while politicians and managers of education systems have the power to offer rewards and to impose sanctions to encourage teachers to innovate, it is teachers themselves who ultimately decide whether or not any innovation will be implemented in classrooms. The problem as we see it is that teachers and those proposing innovations have not in general been able to engage in rational consideration of the costs and benefits implied by innovations because the costs in terms of lost professional craft knowledge and in terms of new craft knowledge to be acquired have not been explicit.

Where it is possible to articulate these costs, as we think we have begun to be able to do, then both parties will be better placed. Innovators can consider ways of modifying their proposals so as to minimize the extent to which teachers would have to change the craft knowledge they use. Teachers will be able to consider the costs that the proposed changes will involve for them, and where they consider such costs acceptable, deliberately to develop the craft knowledge necessary; and they will be able to make clear to others what costs they are carrying.

Implications for the appraisal of experienced teachers

What the appraisal of teachers might involve, and indeed what it should be taken to *mean*, are issues high on the political agenda of British education. Should it incorporate some kind of assessment of *teaching*? Should such assessment be based on observation of the teaching? How much observation would be necessary to allow fair assessment? In what terms should any such assessments be made?

As researchers we are not parties to any negotiation, or any struggle, over such issues. We can, however, hope to provide some relevant information.

First, it is clear from the studies we have reported that the experienced teachers with whom we worked (and, we suspect, most experienced teachers) can and do rely in their day-to-day teaching on a sophisticated knowledge and understanding of the classroom situations with which they have to deal, and on a fluent use of that knowledge and understanding in order to promote and maintain desirable and practicable patterns of classroom activity and various kinds of progress. Any appraisal of teachers which did not take this classroom expertise into account would surely be unbalanced, not to say ridiculous.

Second, it is also apparent that, given appropriate conditions, these teachers (and, again we suspect, the great majority of teachers) are able to articulate clearly and coherently the ways in which they use this professional craft knowledge on any particular occasions. It is not necessary for teaching to remain something mysterious and uncommunicated, or as the charismatic expression and effect of a teacher's 'personality', or alternatively as an unrecognized and unappreciated kind of expertise. It is possible for teachers to show their professional expertise not only by doing their teaching, but also by explaining *what* they have done in their teaching, and *why*. Teachers do not, however, carry their professional craft knowledge around with them, already formulated and available for sharing with others whenever and however it is sought. Their articulation of it is instead a demanding reconstruction of their thinking on particular occasions. Although we have not explored the conditions *necessary* for teachers' articulation of their professional craft knowledge, we know what conditions do make it possible and these are where teachers, treated respectfully in a reflective atmosphere, are encouraged to give their own accounts of lessons which have been observed. Decontextualized accounts, critical questioning, or cross-examination in terms of observers' ideas are most unlikely to contribute usefully to the appraisal of teaching.

Third, it is clear from our studies that teachers' articulation of what they have been doing *is necessary* if their teaching is to be understood. Judgements can clearly be made without the help of teachers' explanations of their own teaching, and we do not suggest that such judgements, by pupils or by observers, are of no value. But for judgements to be based on an understanding of what teachers have been doing, they are necessarily dependent on teachers' explanations of what was happening. Even some-one who is both an experienced teacher and an experienced observer cannot be at all confident of knowing from observation alone what an observed teacher is trying to achieve, what he or she is doing to attain that goal, or the considerations of which the teacher has taken account.

Finally, it is necessary to recognize the diversity of teaching, in two differ-ent ways. On the one hand, teachers differ, not so far as we can tell in the general nature of their professional craft knowledge nor in the general kinds of consideration of which they take account, but to some degree in the patterns of classroom activity and the kinds of progress they seek to promote and in the actions they take to achieve these purposes. Any standardized set of criteria for good teaching would be inadequate to capture the strengths of different teachers. On the other hand, and even more important, for each individual teacher there are different kinds of lesson to be taught, different phases of each type of lesson, and many different circumstances which vary from occasion to occasion and of which account has to be taken in one's teaching. To get a reliable and valid picture of any one teacher's strengths, it is therefore necessary to learn about that teacher's teaching of different kinds of lessons to different classes in different circumstances. In other words, it is necessary to spend a lot of time with that teacher in his or her classroom. In practice, this may imply that it is not practicable for a valid comprehensive appraisal of a teacher's teaching to be made by anyone else. Instead, a teacher who feels defensive or who is suspected of being weak might be asked to identify areas of strength for appraisal, and a confident teacher might volunteer areas of weakness for appraisal.

Looking forward

This research, like other recent studies in North America and Europe, has just begun to reveal the nature, pattern and varieties of teachers' professional craft knowledge. It should be treated as the beginning of a long-term programme. The need now is to pursue in a systematic and more detailed way the kinds of craft knowledge involved in particular modes of teaching specific subjects, and in teaching different age groups.

Summary

In this final chapter, we first concluded from our studies that it *is* possible to gain valid access to teachers' professional craft knowledge, and we summarized what we have found about the nature of teachers' professional craft knowledge. We then returned to some of the practical reasons which we suggested in Chapter 1 for it being important that teachers' craft knowledge should be made explicit. Our findings have confirmed for us the importance of, and helped us clarify the reasons for, beginning teachers gaining access to experienced teachers' craft knowledge; and we mentioned the research on which we are engaged into the facilitation of such access for beginning teachers. Our initial beliefs about the potential for teachers' in-service education of the sharing of professional craft knowledge have also been strengthened by our findings both of the richness of this knowledge and of teachers' experiences of making it explicit. Similarly, it is possible now to say in rather more detail how and why the consideration of teachers' professional craft knowledge could facilitate the planning and introduction of useful curriculum innovations. We have argued too that any attempt at teacher appraisal which ignores the rich, fine-grained and complex professional craft knowledge of the kind we have discovered will inevitably be unproductive. And finally, we have emphasized that in our own judgement the importance of the work reported in this book is that it shows how much we all have still to learn about the complex and subtle professional craft of teaching.

References

Batten, M. (1989). 'Teacher and pupil perspectives on the positive aspects of classroom experience', *Scottish Educational Reviews* 21: 48–57.

Benner, P. (1984). *From Novice to Expert: Excellence and Power in Clinical Nursing Practice*. Menlo Park: Addison-Wesley.

Bensman, J. and Lilienfield, R. (1973). *Craft and Consciousness*. New York: John Wiley.

Berliner, D.C. (1986). 'In pursuit of the expert pedagogue', *Educational Researcher* 15(7): 5–13.

Berliner, D.C. (1988). *The Development of Expertise in Pedagogy*. Charles W. Hunt Memorial Lecture, American Association of Colleges for Teacher Education, New Orleans.

Brophy, J.E. and Good, T.L. (1986). 'Teacher behaviour and student achievement'. In M.C. Wittrock (ed.), *Handbook of Research on Teaching* (3rd edn). New York: Macmillan.

Brown, S. and McIntyre, D. (1988). 'The professional craft knowledge of teachers', *Scottish Educational Review*, Special Issue on The Quality of Teaching, edited by W.A. Gatherer, 39–47.

Calderhead, J. (1981a). 'A psychological approach to research on teachers' classroom decision-making', *British Educational Research Journal* 7: 51–7.

Calderhead, J. (1981b). 'Stimulated recall: a method for research on teaching', *British Journal of Educational Psychology* 51: 211–17.

Calderhead, J. (1990). 'Representations of teachers' knowledge'. In P. Goodyear (ed.), *Teaching Knowledge and Intelligent Tutoring*. New York: Ablex.

Clark, C.M. and Peterson, P.L. (1986). 'Teachers' thought processes'. In M.C. Wittrock (ed.), *Handbook of Research on Teaching* (3rd edn). New York: Macmillan.

Clark, C.M. and Yinger, R.J. (1987). 'Teacher planning'. In J. Calderhead (ed.), *Exploring Teachers' Thinking*. London: Cassell.

Cohen, D. (1977). *Ideas and Action: Social Science and Craft in Educational Practice*. Chicago: Center for New Schools.

Desforges, C. and McNamara, D. (1977). 'One man's heuristic is another man's blindfold: some comments on applying social science to educational practice', *British Journal of Teacher Education* 3(1): 27–39.

Desforges, C. and McNamara, D. (1979). 'Theory and practice: methodological procedures for the objectification of craft knowledge', *British Journal of Teacher Education* 51(2): 145–52.

Doyle, W. (1986). 'Classroom organisation and management'. In M.C. Wittrock (ed.), *Handbook of Research in Teaching* (3rd edn). New York: Macmillan.

Dreyfus, H.L. and Dreyfus, S.E. (1986). *Mind over Machine*. New York: Free Press.

Dunkin, M.J. and Biddle, B.J. (1974). *The Study of Teaching*. New York: Holt, Rinehart and Winston.

Ebel, K.E. (1976). *The Craft of Teaching: A Guide to Mastering the Professor's Art*. San Francisco: Jossey-Bass.

Eisikovits, Z. and Becker, J. (1983). 'Beyond professionalism: the child and youth worker as craftsman', *Child Care Quarterly* 12(2): 93–100.

Eisner, E. (1979). *The Educational Imagination on the Design and Evaluation of School Programs*. New York: Macmillan.

Elbaz, F. (1983). *Teacher Thinking: A Study of Practical Knowledge*. New York: Nichols.

Elliott, J. (1989). 'Appraisal of performance or appraisal of persons'. In H. Simons and J. Elliott (eds), *Rethinking Appraisal and Assessment*. Milton Keynes: Open University Press.

Feiman-Nemser, S. and Buchmann, M. (1985). 'Pitfalls of experience in teacher preparation', *Teachers College Record* 87(1): 53–66.

Fenstermacher, G. (1986). 'Philosophy of research in teaching: three aspects'. In M. C. Wittrock (ed.), *Handbook of Research on Teaching* (3rd edn). New York: Macmillan.

Kohl, H.R. (1976). *On Teaching*. New York: Schocken Books.

Leinhardt, G. and Greeno, J.G. (1986). 'The cognitive skill of teaching', *Journal of Educational Psychology* 78(2): 75–95.

Leinhardt, G. and Smith, D.A. (1985). 'Expertise in mathematics instruction: subject matter knowledge', *Journal of Educational Psychology* 77(3): 247–71.

Lortie, D.C. (1975). *Schoolteacher: A Sociological Study*. Chicago: University of Chicago Press.

McAlpine, A., McIntyre, D., Brown, S. and Hagger, H. (1988). *Student Teachers Learning from Experienced Teachers*. Edinburgh: Scottish Council for Research in Education.

McNamara, D.R. (1980). 'The outsider's arrogance: the failure of participant observers to understand classroom events', *British Educational Research Journal* 6: 113–25.

McNamara, D. and Desforges, C. (1978). 'The social sciences, teacher education and the objectification of craft knowledge', *British Journal of Teacher Education*, 4(1): 17–36.

Marland, M. (1975). *The Craft of the Classroom*. Exeter, NH: Heinemann Educational Books.

Martin, R.J. (1978). 'Craftsmanship and schooling', *Journal of Thought* 13: 187–95.

Morland, P.W. (1977). 'A study of teachers' interactive thoughts', unpublished doctoral dissertation, University of Alberta, Edmonton, Canada.

Morine-Dershimer, G. (1990). *To Think Like a Teacher*, paper delivered at the annual conference of the American Educational Research Association at Boston.

Peterson, P.L. and Clark, C.M. (1978). 'Teachers' reports of their cognitive processes during teaching', *American Educational Research Journal* 15: 555–65.

Roehler, L.R. and Duffy, G.G. (1986). 'What makes one teacher a better explainer than another?', *Journal of Education for Teaching* 12: 173–84.

Schön, D.A. (1983). *The Reflective Practitioner: How Professionals Think in Action*. London: Temple Smith.

Schön, D.A. (1987). *Educating the Reflective Practitioner*. San Francisco: Jossey-Bass.

Shavelson, R.J. and Stern, P. (1981). 'Research on teachers' pedagogical thoughts, judgements, decisions and behaviour', *Review of Educational Research* 51: 455–98.

Shulman, L.S. (1986). 'Those who understand: knowledge growth in teaching', *Educational Researcher* 15(2): 4–14.

Spradley, J.P. (1979). *The Ethnographic Interview*. New York: Holt, Rinehart and Winston.

Stenhouse, L. (1984). 'Artistry and teaching: the teacher as the focus of research and development'. In D. Hopkins and M. Wideen, (eds), *Alternative Perspectives on School Improvement*. Lewes: Falmer Press.

Tom, A. (1980). 'Teaching as a moral craft: a metaphor for teaching and teacher education', *Curriculum Inquiry* 10(3): 317–23.

Tom, A. (1984). *Teaching as a Moral Craft*. New York: Longman.

Wilson, S.M., Shulman, L.S. and Rickert, A.E. (1987). '150 different ways of knowing: representations of knowledge in teaching'. In J. Calderhead (ed.), *Exploring Teachers' Thinking*. London: Cassell.

Wise, A.G. (1978). 'Teacher: automator or craftsperson'. In L. Ruben (ed.), *The In-service Education of Teachers*. Boston: Allyn and Bacon.

Wragg, E.C. and Wood, E.K. (1984). 'Pupil appraisals of teaching'. In E.C. Wragg (ed.), *Classroom Teaching Skills*. Beckenham: Croom Helm.

Name index

Subject index